FINANCIAL
ISSUES
FOR CHURCHES

Church Property
and Legal Stewardship

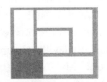

by
Dick L. Kranendonk, Ed.D.

Financial Issues for Churches

Copyright © 2001, Dick L. Kranendonk

ISBN: 1-55306-291-4

Guardian Books is an imprint of *Essence Publishing,* a Christian Book Publisher dedicated to furthering the work of Christ through the written word. For more information, contact: 44 Moira Street West, Belleville, Ontario, Canada K8P 1S3 Phone: 1-800-238-6376 Fax: (613) 962-3055 E-mail: info@essencegroup.com Internet: www.essencegroup.com

Printed in Canada by

Guardian B O O K S

To All
My Colleagues At

CANADIAN COUNCIL
OF
CHRISTIAN CHARITIES

Table of Contents

Preface 11

Who Owns Church Property? 13
   A Church is a Charity 13
   Church Property is Public Property 14
   Church As Fiduciary and Trustee .15
   Church Beneficiaries 16
   Legitimate Uses for Gifts 16
   Conclusion on Property Ownership 17

Member Benefits 19
   Free Facility Use by Members 19
   Benefits Because of Church Membership 20
   Member Participation in Church Programs 20
   Benevolence Fund 21
   Contributors to the Benevolence Fund 22
   Conclusion on Members Benefits 23

Religious Instruction 25
   Church Schools Providing Religious Instruction
      and General Education 25
   Determine Whether a Benefit Results 26
   Determine the Day School Operating Costs 26
   Deduct Non-parent Operating Revenue 27
   Determine Tuition Amount 28
   Determine the Religious-Instruction Cost 29
   Determine the Cost of General Education 31
   Determine the Receiptable Portion of
      Payments by a Parent 32
   Calendar-Year Contributions 32

Church Dinners 33
A Social-Event Dinner 33
A Volunteer-Recognition Dinner 33
An Annual-Meeting Dinner 34
A Fundraising Dinner 35

Contribution Receipts 37
U.S. Charitable Receipts 38
Official Receipts in Canada 38
Receipt Entitlement 41
Golf Tournaments 42

Gifts of Real Estate 43
Gift of a Remainder Interest in
Real Estate - U.S. 44
Gift of a Remainder Interest in
Real Estate - Canada 45
Issues When Accepting Gifts of Real Estate 45

Gifts of Securities 47
Gifts of Publicly-Traded Securities 47
Gifts of Private-Company Shares 48
Other Types of Securities 49
Remainder Interest in Securities 51

Gifts of Life Insurance 55
Term Insurance 55
Whole Life Insurance 56
The Whole-Life Policy Gift 57
The Gift Process and Church Benefit 57
Making the Church the Beneficiary
of a Life Insurance Policy 60

Other Gifts in Kind 61
Gifts of Property vs. Gifts of Services 61

Paying Board Members 65
   Conflict of Interest 66
   The Dual-Board Structure 67
   Some Conflict-of-Interest Situations 69
   Conflict of Pastoral Duties with Trustee Duties 70
   Reimbursement of Expenses 71

Paying Church Staff 73
   Regular Staff Remuneration 73
   Clergy Remuneration 74
   Clergy Housing Allowance 75
   Clergy Residence Deduction 75
   Historical Reason for Clergy Housing Benefits 76

Staff and Volunteer Expenses 79
   Reimbursement for Supplies 79
   Reimbursing Travel 80
   Priority Payments 81
   Benefits of Paying Full Expense Reimbursements 81

Designated Staff Support 83
   Gifts for Public Benefit 83
   Facilitating Personal Gifts 87

Paying Bonuses 91
   Reasonable Remuneration 93

Love Offering 95
   Reasonable Payment Amount .95
   Church Acting as Agent 97
   Withholding Requirements 97
   Canadian Church Love Offering Summary 98

Short-Term Mission Projects 99
   Church-Operated Projects 99
   The Personal Benefit Issue 100

Church-Endorsed Projects 101
Providing Short-Term Mission Bursaries 102

Long-Term Missions 105
Denominational Missions 106
Church Project 106
Agency Arrangement 106
Joint Venture Arrangement 107
Missions Through Other Organizations 109
U.S. Support of Canadian Mission Programs 110

Grants to Foreign Charities 111
U.S. vs. Canadian Law 111
Exceptions for Canadian Churches 112
Conclusion for Canadian Churches 113

Designated Mission Gifts 115
Deputized Fundraising - U.S. 115
Raising Personal Support - Canada 116
Private vs. Public Benevolence 116

General Designated Gifts 119
Conditions for Accepting Designated Gifts 119
Church Policy on Designated Gifts 120

Accepting Bequests 123
Changing a Bequest Designation 123
Enforcing a Church's Rights Under a Will 124
Conclusion on Bequests 125

Borrowing for Operating Purposes 127
Church Revenue Sources 127
Borrowing Purpose 128
Repayment of Loans 128
Borrowing Security 129
Complete Disclosure of Church Assets 129
Liability for Failing to Give Full Asset Disclosure 130

Borrowing for Capital Purposes 131
    Risks of Borrowing for Capital Purposes 132
    Capital Property 132
    Commercial Mortgages 133
    Debenture Financing 134
    Member Loan Financing 136
    Bridge Financing 136
    Combination Financing 137

Borrowing from Restricted Funds 139
    Risks Involved in Borrowing 139
    Inter-Fund Conflict of Interest 140
    Misapplying Funds 141

Investing 143
    Qualified Investments 143
    Prudent Investor Standard 144
    Investment Counsellors and Investment Manager 144
    Need for an Investment Policy 145
    Investment Committee 145
    Investment Policy 146
    Applying Ethical Investment Criteria 147
    The Church and Ethical Investments 148
    Protecting the Church and its Board 149

Permissible Activities 151
    Education Programs 152
    Scholarship and Bursary Programs 152
    Benevolence Programs 153
    Advancing the Gospel Through the Arts 154
    Ancillary Programs 154
    Other Programs 155

Goods and Services Tax 157

Glossary 159

Index 173

Preface

THIS BOOK HAS BEEN WRITTEN to help administrators, treasurers, clergy, elders, deacons, stewards and trustees of churches perform their legal obligations. Administrators of the church's financial affairs who record its receipts and disbursements are usually called treasurers, accountants or business administrators of the church. These employees or volunteers, through the senior pastor as the church's chief executive officer, are ultimately under the governing board's direction and control.

A church's governing board may be the board of elders, the board of deacons, the board of trustees or another like body. Where more than one of these bodies exists in the local church, one or a combination of them is the legal governing body. The issues addressed in this book pertain to the body having final legal authority and accountability over the church's income and assets, as determined in the church's governing documents; however, all others in local church leadership should also be familiar with such issues.

Administrators, treasurers, clergy, deacons, stewards and trustees need to know the legal principles underlying the church's activities in pursuing its charitable purpose. In addition, churches should be able to match the various sources of funds to the different types of expenditures they might incur.

This book was written in response to the many questions received by the Canadian Council of Christian Charities (CCCC) from leaders of churches and related organizations. The enquiries have been collected for several years and relate primarily to four areas: the tax treatment of charities; charitable gifts; receipting issues; and the treatment of gifts, fee income and related borrowing rights of a church.

I am reasonably certain the information in this book is current and accurate at the time of publication; however, tax laws, regulations and administrative practices of government regulators change regularly. I would, therefore, suggest that it be used as a general educational reference tool to help the reader gain a better understanding of charitable principles and related tax issues. This book should not be seen as giving legal or technical advice for specific situations, which should be obtained from independent legal and other appropriate professionals.

Words or phrases that might be unfamiliar to the reader are included in the glossary at the end of the book. The index allows readers to see the use and context of the word or phrase included in the glossary.

Many of the issues addressed are faced by most, if not all, governing boards and financial record keepers of churches and other charities. This book does not address potential legal liability for the church or its governing board. Those issues are covered in my book, *Serving As a Board Member?: Protecting Yourself From Legal Liability While Serving Charities*, (Essence Publishing, Belleville, Ontario, Canada) 1998.

Taxation issues for individual church workers in Canada are not discussed in these pages but are dealt with in the annual *Tax Guide for Religious Workers*. In addition, a more technical book titled *Charities Handbook: Income Tax, Fundraising & Accounting* addresses technical issues applicable to Canadian charities. These two titles are available from the CCCC, 1 - 21 Howard Avenue, Elmira, Ontario, N3B 2C9.

Dick L. Kranendonk, Ed.D.

Who Owns Church Property?

MANY CHURCH PROPERTY AND finance issues are rooted in the question of who owns them. (Church property here means all the resources of the church, not just its real estate.) The immediate response to this question usually is that the property belongs to the church. That is true, but such an answer does not explain on whose behalf the church holds the property.

A church is a not-for-profit entity, meaning it is not operated to earn a profit for its members. As a matter of fact, a church, to be recognized as a charity, must certify that none of its income will be made available to the governing board members (i.e., elders, deacons, stewards, trustees) or to the regular members because of their membership in the church. In other words, the church may not have "shareholders" who have any claim to the church's income or assets.

A Church Is a Charity

But if the church does not hold its property on behalf of its members, for whose benefit is that property held? To answer that, one needs to understand why churches are exempt from income tax and why they are allowed to give receipts for income tax purposes when they receive contributions. It is because all of its resources are to be used only for the charitable purpose for which they were organized—namely the advancement of religion.

Advancement of religion means to teach the church's principles and doctrines to the members and adherents, and to gain converts through mission and evangelism programs. The broad advancement-of-religion purpose is, because of the common law dating back to before the Elizabethan Code of 1601, considered to be charitable. To be charitable a church's objects must benefit the public exclusively.

Church Property is Public Property

The public-benefit requirement means that the church's income and assets, which might have many private-property characteristics, may not be treated by the church or the governing board as private property; instead they are public property.

The term "public property" is most frequently used to describe property controlled by a government or a quasi-government agency. Its meaning, however, should not be restricted by considering who holds the property, but should be understood to encompass all property intended to be used for the public good, rather than for the private benefit of an individual or a group of individuals that can be readily identified.

A church is a charity within the meaning of the common law. Because of this status, the church also receives beneficial tax privileges in two forms. First of all, a church is not taxed on its income. The church's income consists of contributions, return on investment and, in some cases, fees and sales. Secondly, a gift of cash, or other property, made to a church results in a favourable tax treatment for the donor, provided the gifts were made as voluntary transfers for which the donors receive no valuable consideration in return. A church holds all its property (i.e., all its resources including money, physical property and personnel) for the public good to be used exclusively to pursue its religious purpose.

Church As Fiduciary and Trustee

This relationship to the public imposes two restrictions on the board of elders, board of deacons or board of trustees, depending on which one of these bodies has the legal authority over a particular church's income and assets. The first restriction is that the board has fiduciary duties to the church, its members and donors. The second restriction is that the board acts as the trustee for the church's public purpose.

Fiduciaries are persons responsible to deal with entrusted property on behalf of those who have appointed them. For example, a person appointed as another person's power of attorney has fiduciary duties to the one who appointed him/her and must avoid any conflict of interest in dealing with that person's affairs. The fiduciary may not commingle the money belonging to the person who appointed him/her with personal funds. Neither may the person who is power of attorney deal with the property of the one who appointed him/her as if it were his/her own property. The power of attorney also may not do business on behalf of the one who appointed him/her with anyone who is not dealing at arm's length with him/her, except if specifically authorized in the document appointing the power of attorney. A fiduciary is always accountable to the person or group who has appointed the attorney.

A trustee is a person who, in addition to having all the fiduciary duties, has obligations to persons other than those who have appointed him/her. For example, an estate's executor has the fiduciary duties described in the previous paragraph but is not accountable to the person who appointed the executor when a legal document called a *will* was created. To be able to exercise an executor's duties, the testator (i.e., the person who made the will) must have died. The executor's accountability, therefore, is to the will's beneficiaries—those to whom the estate's net assets must be distributed. Accountability to beneficiaries who are distinct from settlors or testators (i.e. those who appointed the executor or trustee) is what makes a person a trustee.

Church Beneficiaries

No one can know the future beneficiaries of a church when it, or the trust creating it, is established. We never know who the Lord will draw to Himself or who will be the ongoing beneficiaries of the Gospel.

The church's governing board is accountable for the use of the church's income and assets as both fiduciary and trustee. The governing board is accountable for its fiduciary duties to those who elected or appointed it to office. The board is accountable for its trustee duties, on behalf of the public beneficiaries, to the representatives of the public. Each legal jurisdiction in the U.S. and Canada has a specific government office, usually the attorney general, which deals with trustee accountability.

Legitimate Uses for Gifts

Members, adherents or visitors have no say over the use of the funds they donate to the church. The legal governing board is elected or appointed to use the income and assets for the church's religious purpose, which must comply with the mission and objects in its governing documents. The church's stated plan for the projects or programs to be undertaken also must agree with its religious purpose.

If the governing board allows funds to be used for purposes other than those authorized in the governing documents, each governing board member is in breach of his/her fiduciary duty to the contributors. Donors who gave to a specific approved project or program of the church can enforce the use of their gifts for the designated program, even if the alternative use is also in pursuit of a charitable purpose.

When a church's governing board is in breach of trust the public's legal representative in the church's jurisdiction can call the governing board to account for alleged improper use of funds. Unauthorized use of property is a misapplication of resources that results in a loss for the rightful owners—the public beneficiaries.

The public's legal representative has the authority to bring charges against the governing board and its individual members under the appropriate statute in the church's jurisdiction. For example, if the church uses funds collected for overseas missions to cover its operating costs at home, the attorney general's department would be able to represent the interests of the donors to the mission funds. The department would charge the church's governing board members with breach of their trustee duties, resulting possibly in a jail sentence and/or a judgment requiring repayment of the funds. Repayments would have to be made by each board member out of his/her personal resources. Since such a court enforced repayment is not made voluntarily, the board members would not be making a charitable gift as will be seen in the next chapter.

Conclusion on Property Ownership

The above discussion shows that the church does not beneficially own the property and resources over which it has control. Rather, the church holds such property *in trust* for the church's public purpose (i.e., the advancement of religion).

Every church board and its individual members should remember the following primary principle in everything that the church does:

The church holds all its resources, including all gifts and other income, in trust for its charitable purpose to promote the church's mission and to gain converts, both locally and globally.

Member Benefits

A COMMON MISCONCEPTION AMONG church members is that the church's property belongs to the congregation, if not themselves. After all, aren't they the ones who have sacrificed for, and contributed to, the church? If the previous chapter was disconcerting to some readers, this one might be even more so.

For a gift to be acceptable as a charitable donation, it must be made voluntarily without valuable consideration of any kind flowing back to the donor. Otherwise the payment is not a gift either under the common law of charity or the income tax statutes of either the U.S. or Canada, and the contributor is not entitled to the favourable tax treatment available for a legitimate gift.

Free Facility Use by Members

For example, if the church allows its members to use its facilities without cost but charges rent to other members of the community, the church member receives a valuable consideration which is a benefit based solely on membership. Similarly, if the church provides benevolence assistance only to its members and not to the adherents or to any other member of the community, a valuable consideration (i.e., a material benefit) is attached to church membership.

Benefits Because of Church Membership

If a church confers any material benefit on its members simply because of their membership, it also is not devoting all its resources exclusively to pursue its charitable purpose. The church could lose its charitable registration number in Canada, or its qualified organization status in the U.S. if found guilty of this by the courts. Such a determination could be devastating for the church, and its donors would no longer be eligible for favourable tax treatment on their contributions. The church, consequently, might be forced to close its doors permanently.

Member Participation in Church Programs

Church members may be beneficiaries of the church's charitable programs as members of the general community, but not because of their membership in the church. This restriction is not intended to be discriminatory against the members. The prohibition exists only in situations where a program's material benefit is restricted to be available only to members at the exclusion of others who would otherwise have a reasonable opportunity to participate.

For example, members of the church gather on the Lord's day to worship and to be nurtured by God's Word. As long as the community is invited to participate in the services, no special benefit is given to the members because of their membership.

Similarly, a church may assist members and adherents to prepare for a career in religious service by awarding scholarships or bursaries. Even though those eligible will be individuals who attend the church, no special benefit is conferred because of church membership. As long as membership is open to all adherents and individuals in the community who are willing to accept the church's membership terms, no objectionable benefit is conferred on the members.

Another example might help to gain a better understanding of the above concepts. Let's assume that a group of seniors wish to set up a recreation club which meets weekly at the church. Since the club is made up exclusively of senior members of the church who live in the seniors' apartments located on church property, the governing board decides that the club may use the facilities free of charge. The reasons for this favourable treatment are,

- the members of the club have been long-time financial contributors to the church;

- undesirable persons will be excluded, because only church members may live in the seniors' apartments.

Clearly the senior members of the church are receiving a material benefit from the church (i.e., the free use of the church's facilities), simply because they are members.

If we, however, take a similar example, and the seniors' club invites any senior in the neighbourhood, or any senior who attends the church, to participate in the club activities, the church is no longer providing a benefit because of membership in the church. Here the free use of the church is legitimately given to the club, because,

- supporting seniors is itself a charitable purpose; and

- the benefit is not restricted to members of the church, but is available to all qualified individuals in the community.

Benevolence Fund

Many churches operate a benevolence fund as part of their ministry activities in pursuing their charitable purpose. These activities are charitable under the categories of the advancement of religion and the relief of poverty. When a church, however, operates a benevolence fund, it does so in obedience to the biblical requirement to look after the poor, the sick, the widow, the orphan and other needy individuals as an act of worship in obedience to the summary of Christ's commandment. The reason for the church establishing a benevolence fund is, therefore, to pursue its religious purpose.

A church's benevolence activities are charitable, even if restricted to those who attend the church, as opposed to members only, provided the church was open for all members of the community to attend without discrimination. If, on the other hand, the benevolence fund will assist only church members, the public benefit requirement will likely not have been met.

Contributors to the Benevolence Fund

The benevolence fund exists to assist all who attend the church and meet the objective criteria for assistance from the fund. Individuals will probably contribute tithes or offerings during the worship service even during times while being assisted by the benevolence fund. These contributions should be accepted as gifts for income tax purposes, and the donor should not be viewed as having received valuable consideration in return.

Further, if the church decides that someone should receive unusually high assistance from its benevolence fund because of disability or disease, it acts within its powers to authorize the related expenditures. Here the church might need to have a special offering during the worship service to raise the required amount. The contributions received during the offering should be treated as valid gifts for income tax purposes. That some worship participants might be related to beneficiaries of the benevolence fund has no bearing on the purpose of the contributions made. The contributors will not be receiving valuable consideration unless the offering mechanism is knowingly used by the contributor to circumvent a prior legal obligation on his/her part to support the recipient of the assistance directly.

Conclusion on Members Benefits

In dealing with which benefits given to members are legitimate, the church should always consider the following questions:

- Is the program, project or privilege resulting in the benefit in accordance with the church's charitable objects?

- Is the program, project or privilege made available to all those who attend the worship services?

- Are the worship services open to everyone in the general community who do not disrupt them?

If the answer to any of these is "no," the benefit would be inappropriate.

Religious Instruction

MOST CHURCHES OFFER INSTRUCTION programs to their members and adherents. The courts have concluded that training programs teaching exclusively the church's confessions, doctrines and practices do not result in a measurable economic or commercial benefit. The benefit of learning about religion is primarily spiritual and does not prepare a person to earn a living, unless it involves post-secondary-level religious training. In the U.S. that concept is entrenched in the separation of church and state doctrine of the Constitution. In Canada that concept is based on the common law.

Church Schools Providing Religious Instruction and General Education

Besides offering a church school program of instruction, some churches also have day school instruction programs during the school year which offer both religious instruction and general education. An economically or commercially measurable benefit is returned to the donor if donors or their children receive general education. General education has commercial or economic value, because it prepares an individual for employment or a career.

Donation receipts a church issues for general education must be only for the portion of contributions to the church which are net of the payment required to cover the cost of the benefit.

This chapter is intended to help churches which operate day schools offering both religious instruction and general education calculate the benefit portion, using the cost-allocation method. Arguably other methods of determining the benefit could be used; however, they would not likely be acceptable to the taxing authorities, at least in Canada. This calculation applies only to elementary and secondary schools. It is assumed that all post-secondary education programs are for direct career preparation in Canada and the U.S.

Determine Whether a Benefit Results

A church charging no fee to parents and not expecting parents to contribute toward the day school program may issue official receipts for the full amount of the contributions made to the church. This approach is available *only* where such a church also does not expect parents who are not members of the church to pay a fee or make contributions for the day school program. It is reasonable to assume that such a church does not provide a consideration because no payment is made by the parents that can be related to the education program. The remainder of this chapter would not apply to such a church.

The rest of this chapter applies to churches that either directly or indirectly charge tuition or expect parents to make donations to the church to fund the day-school program. Even if the contribution is a pledge rather than a fixed fee, a benefit results to the parents because of their contributions.

Determine the Day-School Operating Costs

The first step in determining the benefit portion per student is to separate the operating costs of the day school programs from all other church programs. This can best be done by deducting from the total disbursements in the year all payments made for capital purposes and expenditures incurred for all programs not forming part of the day school program.

Note that capital expenditures include funds used to make investments and payments of principal and interest on loans and mortgages in addition to the cost of buildings, equipment, furniture and fixtures. Anything that is useable for more than twelve months may be treated as a capital expenditure. Capital expenditures include such items as textbooks, library books and computer software—even if expensed in the church's books when acquired. Capital expenditures for the purpose of this calculation includes depreciation and bad debts because such expenditures are not current operating expenditures and should not be included in current operating expenses of the day school program.

Example:

A church operates a day school program in addition to operating several other local ministry and missions programs. Let us assume that the church's total budget is $910,000, that capital purchases and expenditures amount to $60,000 and that all the programs not relating to the day-school program cost $400,000.

Gross Expenditures of the Church		$910,000
Less: Capital Expenditures	60,000	
and Non-School Operations	400,000	460,000
Day-School Operating Costs		$450,000

Deduct Non-Parent Operating Revenue

The church receives operating contributions from both members and adherents who have no children enrolled in the day school. The church may also receive contributions above tuition for the day-school program from parents which should also be classified as non-parent school operating revenue. The church needs to determine the amount of its total non-parent revenue for its general budget that it uses to support the day-school program.

The church might also receive grants from foundations and other charities in support of its day-school program. Some government funds for the day-school program might also be available. The church needs to determine the total of external grants and contributions it receives for school-operating purposes.

Example:

The Church in our example has total day-school operating costs of $450,000. Grants received from foundations, other charities and governments amount to $80,000. Parents with children in the school contribute above tuition amounts of $20,000. The calculation to be made is as follows:

Day-School Operating Costs		$450,000
Less:		
Foundation and Charity Grants	$ 80,000	
Parent Contributions		
(Above Tuition Amount)	20,000	100,000
Cost to be Covered by Tuition		$350,000

Determine the Tuition Amount

Most churches that charge a fixed tuition fee per child would operate their day schools on the basis that tuition fees should cover the day-school operating costs not covered by operating revenue coming from other sources as calculated above. If no fixed tuition is charged, but parents are expected to make contributions in any way, the cost to be covered by tuition would be divided by the number of students enrolled in the day school to arrive at the notional tuition fee.

Example:

Using the same example as noted above, assume that 100

28

children are enrolled in the day school. The tuition per child, whether fixed or notional, will be as follows:

Cost to be Covered by Tuition	$350,000	= $3,500
Number of Children in School	100	

Determine the Religious-Instruction Cost

As noted above, religious instruction at the elementary and secondary school level does not confer a benefit on a child or the child's parents. Churches operating day schools usually teach children more than the general education subjects. They also teach subjects and engage in activities going beyond those of publicly-funded schools (e.g. religious instruction). Religious-instruction time may include time for devotions, teaching Bible, choral music, religious history, religious family studies, world religions, chapel, choral festivals, student and faculty retreats for religious purposes, time to prepare for such religious activities, preparation and marking of assignments for religious subjects, religious counselling and preparation time to integrate the church's confessions, principles and practices into the general education curriculum. Religious-instruction costs, if reasonably distinguishable from costs of general education subjects and activities, may be excluded from the amount resulting in a material benefit for the child because of the general education received.

The greatest cost incurred by a church-operated day school is that of salaries. To determine religious-instruction and general-education costs, it is necessary to calculate the salaries for teaching each. These calculations should be based on time sheets filled out by teachers. An acceptable sample time sheet is as follows:

Classroom Teacher Time Allocation Sheet
(allocated in minutes)
For the Week Ending _____, 200__

Activity	Mon	Tue	Wed	Thur	Fri	Sat/Sun	Total
General Education:							
Teaching English/Language Arts	___	___	___	___	___	___	___
Teaching History/Geography	___	___	___	___	___	___	___
Teaching Mathematics	___	___	___	___	___	___	___
Teaching Science	___	___	___	___	___	___	___
Teaching Modern Languages	___	___	___	___	___	___	___
Teaching Social Studies	___	___	___	___	___	___	___
Teaching Phys. Ed.	___	___	___	___	___	___	___
Teaching Music/Art/Drama	___	___	___	___	___	___	___
Teaching Practical Arts	___	___	___	___	___	___	___
General Counselling	___	___	___	___	___	___	___
General Education	___	___	___	___	___	___	___
Professional Development	___	___	___	___	___	___	___
General Education							
Preparation and Marking	___	___	___	___	___	___	___
A. Subtotal General Education	___	___	___	___	___	___	___
Religious Instruction:							
Worship/Chapel/Devotions	___	___	___	___	___	___	___
Teaching Bible	___	___	___	___	___	___	___
Teaching Choral Music	___	___	___	___	___	___	___
Teaching Religion	___	___	___	___	___	___	___
Teaching Rel. Family Studies	___	___	___	___	___	___	___
Teaching Church History	___	___	___	___	___	___	___
Teaching Ancient Languages	___	___	___	___	___	___	___
Religious Counselling	___	___	___	___	___	___	___
Religious Integration Into							
General -Education Courses	___	___	___	___	___	___	___
Religious Instruction							
Preparation and Marking	___	___	___	___	___	___	___
Religious Instruction							
Professional Development	___	___	___	___	___	___	___
B. Subtotal Religious Instruction	___	___	___	___	___	___	___

C. Total Employment Time (Sum of A and B Subtotal) ___

Percentage Religious Instruction (B divided by C times 100) ___ %

_____
Signature of Teacher

_____
Signature of Principal

Each classroom teacher's salary would be split according to the time sheets and allocated to either the school's religious instruction or general education salary accounts.

All the classroom-teacher's salaries should be allocated to the appropriate accounts. After totalling the religious instruction salaries, other indirect costs should be determined on the basis of the appropriate percentage of total salaries allocated to religious instruction and general education. The resulting percentages should be used to allocate all remaining expenditures (i.e., administrative salaries, benefits, building, maintenance, supplies, and utilities) to either religious instruction or general education.

Determine the Cost of General Education

In the foregoing section, determining the cost of providing the religious instruction of church-operated day schools was discussed. Here the assumption will be that giving religious instruction equals 20% of classroom teacher salaries. Since this percentage applies to all remaining costs, all school-operating expenditures for religious instruction also equal 20%. After ascertaining that, the amount relating to general education remains. Working further with the earlier example, the following determination can be made:

Example:	
Cost to be covered by tuition	$350,000
Less: Cost of religious instruction	90,000
Cost of general education	$260,000

Using the same average number of children enrolled in the day school as used to calculate tuition (i.e., 100 children), the benefit amount per child will be:

$$\frac{\text{Cost of general education}}{\text{Number of children enrolled}} = \frac{\$260,000}{100} = \$2,600$$

31

Determine the Receiptable Portion of Payments by a Parent

The portion of the amount paid by a parent to the church that may be acknowledged with a receipt needs to be calculated next. The total of the receipt would be the parents' contributions to the church less the material benefit received by the parents' children for the general education given by the church's day school.

Example:

Assume 2.5 children (i.e., two children attending the full calendar year and one child finishing at the end of June of the same year).

Total parent operating contributions	$10,000
Less: $2,600 times 2.5 full-time equivalent children	6,500
Gift portion of parent's contributions to the church	$ 3,500
(If the result is negative, enter $0.00)	
Add: Any contributions made in the year for capital purposes	500
Receiptable portion of all contributions	$ 4,000

Calendar-Year Contributions

When parents have children enrolled in a newly established church-operated school, the church must base its calculations to determine the receiptable portion of contributions made prior to December 31st on the disbursements actually made during that calendar year. In all other circumstances the benefit portion of the contributions is determined by using the cost of general education per child for the school year that was completed during the calendar year.

Church Dinners

FROM TIME TO TIME MANY CHURCHES hold dinners for various reasons. They might be appropriate, or they could result in technical difficulties for the church or the dinner participants. The issues to be considered when holding a church dinner are:

- What is the purpose for having the dinner, and

- Who are the invited participants.

A number of situations involving church dinners and how they might affect the church and its members will be discussed.

A Social-Event Dinner

Sometimes churches hold dinners for which they use their own funds, simply as a social event. If only members and donors are invited, a material benefit is received by the members. The church may not give any valuable consideration to the members simply because of their membership.

A charitable purpose is not pursued when a dinner is available simply for social reasons. There must be a religious purpose for all activities undertaken by the church. Further, even if there is a religious reason to hold the dinner but it is available only the church's members and donors, its recognition as a charity could be in jeopardy because a benefit is being given for membership or a benefit is given in return for contributions. Also, a gift made to the church by any participant at the dinner could be challenged. This could happen if the church did not clearly identify and/or deduct the fair market value of the dinner from the amount donated to arrive at the receiptable amount.

A Volunteer-Recognition Dinner

Sometimes the church holds and pays for a dinner to recognize all volunteers who have contributed their time and talents for the various ministries of the church. This dinner would be appropriate, since it recognizes those who have worked diligently in activities that pursue the church's charitable purpose. Technically, the dinner is a form of remuneration which the recipients would have to report as income for tax purposes; however, since the dinner is consumed on site, and assuming that the volunteers do not receive any other material benefit, the taxation authorities would probably treat it like an annual Christmas gift of nominal value.

Any gift made by participants to the church to help defray the cost of the dinner would be charitable and, therefore, entirely receiptable for income tax purposes.

An Annual-Meeting Dinner

Sometimes a church holds a meeting with a dinner, for which it pays, to present its annual report and to approve the coming year's budget. All the members, adherents and donors are encouraged to attend, so that they will take greater ownership of the church's mission and programs. The church's governing board concluded that the dinner would increase participation and would be an opportune time for members to invite a neighbour or a friend. Thus the primary purpose of the dinner is ministry.

In such a situation no concerns exist because the activity is for a charitable purpose in pursuit of the church's objects as recorded in its governing documents. Any gift made by a participant at the dinner would appear to be fully receiptable.

A Fundraising Dinner

The church might also hold a fundraising dinner to receive gifts, or pledge commitments, for the operating budget or a special program such as its outreach mission. Whether the church pays for the dinner or whether some of the invited guests are asked to defray the costs by sponsoring tables, the dinner is for a charitable purpose.

Fundraising activities are charitable, because their purpose is to raise funds so that the church's programs and projects can be maintained or expanded. Any payment made by a participant is partly for food consumed at the dinner and partly a gift. Also, any participant's donation made at the dinner, regardless of whether the table had been paid for by another person, would partly reflect the consumed dinner's cost. The sponsor of the table would be considered to have received valuable consideration for the sponsorship fee of the meal's fair market value times the number of immediate family members participating in the dinner.

In the U.S. the church would have to show the fair market value of the meal on the receipt, as well as the total contributed. The donor would be entitled to claim a deduction from income for the amount donated less the fair market value of the meal.

In Canada the donor would be entitled to receive an official receipt for the gift's net value after the meal's fair market value was deducted.

Note: A fundraising meal's fair market value is its menu price at a local restaurant, not its cost to the church of providing the meal, nor the amount paid by the table's sponsor.

Contribution Receipts

A CHURCH MAY ACKNOWLEDGE contributions received from its members, adherents and visitors with an income tax receipt when the church is satisfied that the donor has not received, nor will receive, any valuable consideration or benefit in return.

Obviously all donors to a church receive a benefit, because they are able to attend and participate in the church's worship services and educational programs. These benefits, however, are not because of membership in the church. Participation in worship services and educational programs are open to all in the community. All those invited are considered to be the potential beneficiaries of the church's ministries. That certain members of the public might not be beneficiaries is their choice, not the church's.

The law does not require that those of the public who make voluntary financial contributions to the church be discriminated against. Discrimination would result if donors were denied the right to the benefit of participating in the church's programs and services. Provided donors receive that benefit together with those of the general community not choosing to make donations, no valuable consideration is conferred. For a more detailed discussion of benefits to members, see the chapter "Member Benefits."

The first concern in this chapter is not the broad benefit available to the community as a whole, but the receipting issues when valuable consideration is available only in return for making a specific gift or for being a member of the church. The second concern is the receipt itself.

U.S. Charitable Receipts

The U.S. *Internal Revenue Code* allows churches to issue written statements, usually called receipts, for all payments made including the identified amounts for which the donors have received valuable consideration. This practice is sometimes referred to as split receipting. For example, parents' contributions to a church might include payments for their children's enrollment in its day school. As long as the U.S. church identifies the payment's tuition portion on the parent's receipt, the parent will be able to claim a taxable-income deduction for the remainder as a gift to the church. Similarly, if a U.S. taxpayer's contribution to a church includes a payment for a book purchased from the church's bookstore and a contribution for the church's programs, only one receipt showing the book's value and the gift amount needs to be issued.

A U.S. church does not have to determine the fair market value of the valuable consideration received by a donor if it is less than 2% of the donation or $74.00. If a contribution is at least $37, a U.S. church may give the donor an item bearing the church's name or logo if the item's cost to the church does not exceed $7.40. (The amounts quoted in this paragraph are for 2000 and might for later years be adjusted for inflation.)

Official Receipts in Canada

In Canada the treatment of a payment that is partly a gift and partly a payment for a purchase of goods or services is much more complex. The basic rule under Canadian income tax law is that if the contributor receives any valuable consideration because of a single payment to the church, the total payment is denied as a gift for income tax purposes.

The few administrative exceptions that the Canada Customs and Revenue Agency has provided over the years are published in interpretation bulletins and information circulars.

These exceptions are:

• Admissions to, or participation in, a fundraising dinner, a place of amusement or like event. Administratively the agency's view on fundraising dinners is that a person consumes, and does not take away, the consideration at that event. Provided the participant does not have the opportunity to "earn" any right or privilege that could be used at another time, the revenue agency allows Canadian registered charities, including churches, to issue official income tax receipts which exclude from total payments the benefit's fair market value. For example, a Canadian church putting on a fundraising dinner costing it $5.00 per plate, where a local restaurant would charge $15.00 for a similar plate, would be able to issue an official receipt for the donated amount less the $15.00 value of the dinner. For example, if the donation was $50.00, the receipt would be for $35.00.

• The revenue agency also allows an official receipt to be issued to donors who receive a nominal inducement in return. A donor may receive an item whose fair market value is the lesser of 10% of the gift or $50.00. Again the value is not the cost to the church for the inducement, but the fair market value (i.e., the cost of a similar consideration if purchased at a local commercial establishment). This consideration-value limit also applies to prizes awarded at special events like golf tournaments, where the prizes' fair market value would have to be within the lesser of 10% of the total payment's gift portion after deducting the golfing fees or $50.00.

- The third exception relates to contributions made by parents and guardians to religious schools in which their children are enrolled and the portion that cannot be receipted. The revenue agency has published two formulae to be used by religious schools and churches with day schools to make this calculation. See the chapter "Religious Instruction."

Aside from the exceptions noted above, the revenue agency will likely deny any contribution as a gift for income tax purposes if other forms of valuable consideration not freely available to the general public are available to the donor. Even if the gift is many times the valuable consideration or benefit received, the total payment will be rejected by the revenue agency as a gift for income tax purposes. Canadian courts have confirmed this *all-or-nothing* approach. In Canada a donor should separate payments for things resulting in valuable consideration from gift payments to the church.

As mentioned the IRS requires U.S. charities to show on a split receipt the payment received from the donor as well as the amount and description, if any, for which the person received valuable consideration. This allows the IRS to easily determine whether the valuable consideration amount identified on the receipt is reasonable. If the amount appears unreasonable, the IRS would have direct recourse to the taxpayer.

In Canada the regulations under the *Income Tax Act* stipulate the content of an official receipt issued by a charity. No other information should be included. Since only the gift amount may be shown on the official receipt, the revenue agency cannot determine from it whether the amount calculated as valuable consideration is reasonable. Consequently the church has a greater onus to make certain that any official receipt complies with all the *Income Tax Act* requirements and the revenue agency's administrative practices.

A Canadian church that issues an official income tax receipt for a payment for which the donor has received valuable consideration risks having its charitable registration number revoked and having to turn all its net assets over to another registered charity within one year of the revocation notice. Any assets remaining in the deregistered church's name after that year would be subject to a 100% penalty tax payable to the revenue agency.

Receipt Entitlement

Another question often asked is whether a receipt may be issued to someone other than the person who made the contribution. For example, an individual owner of an incorporated business might attach a note to the payment from the corporation, requesting that the church make the receipt out to an individual. The communication states that the corporation is treating the payment as personal income to the individual on the books of the corporation. The individual, therefore, wishes to receive the receipt for tax purposes personally. The church would have no way to verify that the amount donated was actually treated as income received from the corporation by the individual. For that reason the taxation authorities insist the receipt be made out in the name of the person who made the payment. If the payment is made by a corporation, the receipt must be issued in the corporation's name.

The issue would be the same when one individual makes a donation and then asks the church to issue the charitable donation receipt to someone else. The church must be able to show in its financial records that it issued the receipt to the individual who made the contribution.

To avoid any misunderstanding about the name to be recorded on the receipt, the church should contact the donor before depositing the donation in its bank account. The church should explain that it is entitled to issue a receipt only to the person who made the payment. If the donor insists on having the receipt issued in another person's name, the contribution should be returned. The individual will then be able to issue a new cheque drawn on his/her personal bank account.

Golf Tournaments

In Canada a frequent example of dual receipting occurs at fundraising golf tournaments which have been popular for church and para-church organizations. A donor participating in a church golf tournament normally pays more for participating than the golfing fees would otherwise be. The golfers, however, unquestionably receive valuable consideration for the admission to the tournament. The donor/golfer also knows that a contribution to a church project is included in the admission charge.

Since the golf tournament is classified by the Canadian revenue agency as an event similar to a fundraising dinner, the tax treatment for such payments are the same for Canadian churches as for U.S. churches. The payments consist of two components: a gift portion and a fee portion. The golfer/donor is entitled to an official receipt for that portion of the payment exceeding the fair market value of the normal green fees and a noncharitable receipt for the portion representing the fair market value of the green fees.

If, however, the golfer/donor has the opportunity to "earn" any other benefit at the golf tournament, the total payment made is not a gift. For example, the revenue agency has issued an interpretation bulletin stating in part that the right to "earn" a prize if a person makes a "hole-in-one" will be sufficient to deny any portion of the payment made to participate in the golf tournament as a gift. The IRS would not likely take this restrictive approach, but a U.S. church should consult with a professional before organizing such an event.

Gifts of Real Estate

CHURCHES ARE BEING CONTACTED more often by members wishing to donate property other than cash. Such a donation is called a "gift in kind," the most common of which is real property.

When a donor expecting to receive an income tax receipt offers a church real property, the church should be aware of its responsibilities. What value should the church report on a receipt for a gift that was not received in the form of cash?

A real estate gift's value can be difficult to determine. For example, the real property might be located in a remote region where few properties change hands. The donor might wish to contribute the real estate so the church can establish a children's camp outreach mission subject to approval by the church's leadership and membership. The church should obtain an appraisal of the real property from a qualified, independent real estate appraiser (i.e., one dealing with the church and the donor at arm's length by not being related to the donor nor to any other member of the church's governing board). The appraiser takes all facts relating to the property and its proposed use into account. His/her ascertained value may be accepted as the real estate's true fair market value. Some professionals, however, suggest that the church should obtain at least two independent appraisals prepared by qualified individuals. The fair market value would be the average of the two appraisals.

Gifts of mortgaged real estate needs to be considered before being accepted. If a mortgage exists on property given to a U.S. church by a U.S. taxpayer, the receipt the church issues should report the property's fair market value and the mortgage mount, so the donor can arrive at the charitable gift's net value.

In Canada no consideration from a gift may accrue to the donor. Since the mortgage indebtedness is an obligation distinct from the real estate (i.e., the real estate is only the security given for the loan) the transfer of the real estate with the mortgage security attached would result in consideration given back to the donor. Once title to the real property is transferred, the donor could stop making payments on the mortgage loan. Then the lending institution would lay claim to the real property that had been assigned as security for the loan. Because of this possibility, the donor would have received consideration for having made the gift (i.e., the funds obtained on the real property's security). As a consequence of Canadian tax law, a gift of real estate to a Canadian church may be recognized as a gift for income tax purposes only where the mortgage is paid off before title to the property is transferred.

Another method of donating real estate occurs when a senior couple wish to give their home to the church of which they are members, while retaining the right to continue living in the home until the last surviving donor dies or is no longer able to live there. This gift in kind is a gift of a remainder interest in the home. The church should be aware of special rules before accepting the gift of a home on such terms.

Gift of a Remainder Interest in Real Estate - U.S.

In the U.S. donors are entitled to claim for income tax purposes a gift as a deduction from taxable income equal to the remainder interest in the home. The remainder interest is calculated based on the present fair market value of the home discounted for the remainder interest in the property on the assumed future possession date. Title in the home would be transferred to the church at the time the arrangement was made; however, the church would not be able to take possession of the home until the last surviving spouse dies or has moved out permanently. The IRS accepts the life expectancy on the joint lives as the church's estimated possession date. It requires the current value of the home on the estimated possession date to be discounted. It prescribes a formula for calculating the value of the remainder interest. Two prescribed factors in the formula are an approved rate of interest and the number of years until the estimated possession date.

Gift of a Remainder Interest in Real Estate - Canada

The same approach is applicable in Canada. A church in Canada would also be entitled to issue an official receipt for income tax purposes to donors who transferred title of their home to the church. The receipt's value would be calculated similarly to that in the U.S.

Issues When Accepting Gifts of Real Estate

Besides the income tax consequences, churches should be aware of other issues, one of which is whether the church wishes to be a landlord. When donors retain the right to live in their homes for the rest of their lives, several things need to be addressed, some of which include the following:

- Who will be responsible for paying the property taxes on the home or other real property if the church has received the transfer of title but has not yet received the right to possess the property?

- Who will be responsible to pay for the property and casualty insurance when the property is transferred to the church but not yet in complete possession of the church?

- Who will be responsible for the maintenance costs of the home or other real property before the church receives the right to actually occupy the property?

Regarding real property that is not a private residence, the church should consider the following:

- What does the church wish to do with the property?

- Are there any restrictions on the property's use that could pose problems for the church?

- Are there any environmental concerns with the property?

The church should exercise special care regarding potential environmental concerns. Upon transfer of the real estate title to the church, it becomes liable for all problems relating to the property. Situations have occurred where environmental clean-up costs far exceeded the property's value. The church's governing board deciding to accept a gift of real estate would show prudence and care in having the donor obtain an environmental-clearance certificate before accepting such property.

Gifts of Securities

FROM AN INCOME TAX PERSPECTIVE, shares of corporations and other similar securities are attractive for Canadians and Americans to donate to a church as gifts in kind. Pitfalls, however, exist in accepting some instruments classified as securities. Securities normally include, among other more sophisticated instruments, common and preferred shares of both private and public corporations, mutual or other pooled fund units, and debt instruments such as bonds and debentures.

Gifts of Publicly-Traded Securities

Since securities are property rather than services, they can be accepted as charitable gifts by a church, as long as it can determine the securities' fair market value. To determine the fair market value of common and preferred shares or mutual fund and index units listed on a stock exchange is relatively simple. The closing value of a stock reported in the newspaper on the day the gift is made would be the acceptable value for receipting purposes. Similarly, most mutual funds and other pooled funds publicly report the daily closing value of their units. The value of many bonds and other debt instruments also can be determined via daily newspaper reports.

The question arises as to when a gift of securities is actually made. As a general rule a gift of cash is not completed until the church has accepted it. On the face of it this appears true for a gift of securities as well. An exception to the general rule is made for a year-end gift made by mail. In a year-end gift made by mail the transaction is considered to have been completed when it has been deposited in a mail box. The postmark on the envelope is accepted as evidence that the gift was made. The same timing approach would appear acceptable for gifts of securities. The date on which donors of securities give written instructions to their brokers to irrevocably transfer the ownership of shares or other securities traded on a stock exchange to the church without further conditions or restrictions attached to the transfer should be accepted as the date on which the gift was made. The fair market value of the securities for receipting purposes, therefore, should be the closing value on the day the donor irrevocably transferred them to the church.

Gifts of Private-Company Shares

To establish the value of shares not listed on a stock exchange such as shares of a private corporation, requires an independent appraisal by a qualified person dealing at arm's length with the donor and the church.

A transfer of private corporation shares to a church in Canada is classified as a non-qualified security. A donor retaining control of the private corporation after the shares have been transferred is not entitled to an income tax receipt until the shares have been disposed of by the charity. The disposition must take place within sixty months from the date of transfer to the church. The shares of a private corporation donated to a charity will be deemed to have been disposed of by the charity at the death of the donor if death occurs within sixty months after the gift was made. If the shares have not been disposed of within sixty months, no official receipt may ever be issued by the church. If the shares are disposed of, the official receipt will be for the proceeds that the church receives.

The donor could incorporate a new corporation to become the owner of the existing private corporation's shares the donor wishes to donate to a church. Provided the donor made a gift of all the new corporation's outstanding shares, an income tax receipt for their fair market value (established by an independent appraiser) could be issued immediately. This value of the new company shares will, of course, be equal to that of the shares it holds in the existing private corporation.

A gift of securities described in the previous paragraphs is very sophisticated. Before the church accepts them, it should obtain professional advice. There are also potential serious tax consequences for the donor if independent professional advice is not obtained by the donor. Only the well-informed donor should consider making a gift of securities in a private corporation, and a church should only accept such a gift when it is clear how or when it can be converted to cash.

Other Types of Securities

Other very complicated securities include units in hedge funds and units in limited partnerships that do not trade on a stock exchange. Such securities are also at times offered to charities. Although these securities are property in the legal sense of the word, a church should not accept them without obtaining, with assistance from appropriate professionals, answers to the following:

• Can the security's fair market value be established?

   If not, the charity should not issue an income tax receipt to the donor.

• Are there redemption restrictions attached to the security?

If the issuing corporation will not redeem the security within a reasonable time and no secondary market for it exists, the security's value is probably nominal.

- Is there any remaining obligation to make future additional payments to the issuer of the security?

Units in some limited partnerships and some hedge funds are frequently sold where the purchaser makes a small cash payment and the issuer takes back what is often referred to as a "no recourse promissory note" for the remainder. The security issued in effect secures such a note. The investment's primary value for the original purchaser is the high tax write-offs available in the early years. The original investor's exposure normally is more than offset by the generous tax write-offs enjoyed. The secondary value is the less certain prospect of the underlying venture being successful. A U.S. church should be very loath to accept such a security as a gift because of the difficulty in determining net value. In Canada such a security would not qualify as a gift since the debt of the original note held by the donor would be extinguished, constituting consideration being returned to the donor.

- Would there be a danger that ownership of such securities results in the church being involved in a business, rather than a passive investment?

The profits and losses of the underlying business activity for many limited partnership and hedge fund units flow through to the unit holders. That is the very feature which makes the units attractive to the original investor, but that could mean the church would be earning profit from a business venture rather than a passive investment, resulting in the church being required to file a tax return in the U.S. and to pay tax on the profit realized. For a Canadian church the question arises whether the charity is devoting all its resources exclusively to its charitable purpose, because a Canadian charity may not be involved in a business activity not directly related to its charitable purpose. Churches having a "flow-through" of profits and losses from the underlying business activity are exposed to business risk. If the church does not receive with the units the right *and* opportunity to immediately sell them, the church and its governing board, upon acceptance, might expose themselves to unnecessary liability even if the fair market value is established by an independent, qualified appraiser.

Although donating a security can be very attractive to the donor because of favourable tax treatment, a church should be prudent in deciding whether to accept such contributions.

Remainder Interest in Securities

Frequently donors wish to receive income earned by the church from the donated securities for the rest of their lives. This can be accomplished through a charitable remainder trust, also known as an irrevocable trust. The donor is usually the settlor (sometimes called the "trustor") and income beneficiary and the church is the trustee and usually the capital beneficiary.

A trust, to be a valid trust, must have a settlor, a trustee, and one or more beneficiaries. The charitable remainder trust's settlor irrevocably transfers (donates) property to the trust to benefit the income and capital beneficiaries. The settlor would be the income beneficiary. The trustee (i.e., the church) receives the property from the settlor and holds it in trust for the benefit of the capital beneficiary (i.e., the church) and the income beneficiary (i.e., the settlor) until the settlor's death. The church will not possess the capital contributed to the trust for its own use until the trust property passes from the trust to the church at the settlor's death.

When a charitable remainder trust is established to hold securities, the settlor transfers the securities, which the settlor intends to give to the church, to the trustee to hold in trust for the two beneficiaries. Both publicly-traded and private-company shares or other forms of securities can be transferred to a charitable remainder trust. The settlor will receive the periodic dividend or interest income until death. The church receives the securities upon the death of the settlor.

Such a trust arrangement usually is attractive to the donor for the following reasons:

- The gift of securities irrevocably transferred to a trust passes to the beneficiary outside the estate. For U.S. settlors such gifts are not subject to estate tax.

- A gift by trust is not subject to probate. A trust is a private document, which, therefore, reduces the potential for challenging the gift as might happen with a bequest by will.

- Since the church does not possess the securities until the settlor's death, nothing prevents issuance of an income tax receipt in Canada when private-company shares or debt instruments are transferred to a trust. Although they are non-qualified securities, they can be disposed of by the church as soon as it receives them following the settlor's death. Often the settlor will arrange a life insurance policy owned by the private corporation, so the insurance proceeds it receives upon the settlor's death may be used to redeem the shares or the debt instrument held by the trust. Using a charitable remainder trust enables the settlor to contribute non-qualified securities and immediately receive an official receipt for the remainder interest's fair market value. That the church may issue the receipt only when the remainder value can be established with some certainty should be noted. Determining the fair market value of the remainder interest for private corporation shares might be difficult, unless insurance is in place. Without this certainty, Canadian tax authorities might challenge the validity of the remainder interest as a gift.

• Where the remainder interest's fair market value can be reasonably established, the donor is entitled to an income tax receipt for the gift's present value, determined by discounting the value of the securities based on the settlor's actuarial life expectancy.

Because they are legal entities distinct from the settlor and the church, charitable remainder trusts are relatively complex instruments, requiring ongoing reporting to government authorities. A church should be satisfied that it has the expertise to handle arrangements like this before agreeing to enter them. Churches deciding to do so should first obtain professional advice and assistance.

Gifts of Life Insurance

LIFE INSURANCE POLICIES ALSO CAN be used for making gifts in kind. The life insurance industry as well as some charities frequently promote such policies, which are property transferrable to churches or other charities. A church should be educated about life insurance policy gift programs before encouraging its members to participate in them. Two basic types of life insurance policies exist. One type is called "term insurance." The other is usually referred to as "whole life insurance."

Term Insurance

Often term insurance is purchased to insure, for instance, mortgage debt if the insured debtor dies. This prevents the mortgage from having to be repaid by the borrower's dependents out of future income. Sometimes term insurance is purchased to support dependents in case the insured person dies before the dependents are able to look after their own financial needs.

As the name "term insurance" implies, the coverage is available for a contracted number of years. At the end of each year, the premium equals the insurance protection received. No value, therefore, can be receipted when a term insurance policy's ownership is transferred to a church. The church will benefit only if the insured person dies before the policy expires, provided the periodic premium payments have been made.

Whole Life Insurance

Whole life insurance, on the other hand, guarantees that the insurance will remain in force for the insured's lifetime as long as the minimum required premium payments have been made. Whole life insurance has two elements: pure insurance protection and a savings feature. The savings feature produces the whole life policy's cash-surrender value. When a whole life policy is purchased, its face value is guaranteed if the premium payments are made according to the policy contract.

The insurance company sets the periodic premium payments by estimating the future costs of maintaining the policy in force. The future costs include the anticipated economic climate, the cost of the policy payout (i.e., the anticipated mortality rate) and the profit the insurance company wishes to earn for entering into the policy contract. These variables are sometimes referred to as the insurance company's risks. Since such risks are constantly subject to change, the insurance company sets the periodic premium payments significantly higher than would be required to maintain pure insurance. The premium payments must contain a fair amount to cover the risks of changing conditions. In addition the insurance company usually contracts with the policy owner that premium payments will terminate before the insured individual's life expectancy. When premium payments are no longer required the policy is said to be "paid up."

The premium payment amount above the cost of pure insurance produces the "cash-surrender value." The cash-surrender value consists of the paid-up amount (i.e., the amount reserved within the policy to maintain it after premium payments cease) and the accumulated "dividends."

An insurance policy's dividends are not normally earnings produced by the investment of excess premium payments.

Rather, they represent the excess premium payments made (i.e., the amount in excess of the actual costs of maintaining the policy to maturity). These dividend payments are, therefore, a return of the policy owner's excess premium payments and are not taxable when received.

The Whole-Life Policy Gift

A donation of a whole life policy to the church effectively is a gift of the cash-surrender value, including the accumulated excess premium payments made to the insurance company. By changing the policy's beneficiary and transferring ownership of the policy to the church, the church becomes owner of the cash-surrender value, including the accumulated dividends. The policy's donor is entitled to receive a charitable receipt for the policy's cash-surrender value, because the church would be able to surrender the insurance policy to the insurance company and receive the cash-surrender value.

The Gift Process and Church Benefit

As shown above, to donate a whole life insurance policy that has served its original purchase purpose is beneficial. To donate a term insurance policy to a church or other charity, however, is not sensible.

Once the church has received a life insurance policy as a gift, the church needs to determine whether to retain the policy or to surrender it to the insurance company for the cash-surrender value including the accumulated excess premium payments. A church deciding to keep the policy might have to make additional premium payments. Whether making these payments is wise depends partly on the policy and partly on the donor's restrictions when the gift was made.

For example, assume the donor makes no restrictions by

allowing the church to do with the policy what it thinks is best. The church should determine whether the additional accumulation of funds within the policy (assuming no additional premium payments will be made) would be greater than the return that could be generated by the built-up capital in another secure investment. If the latter is true, and it usually is, the policy should be surrendered for its built-up capital, and the proceeds should be invested in the other investment.

Another example is when the donor requests the church to keep the policy in force and guarantees to make sufficient additional premium payments directly to the insurance company on behalf of the church. Alternatively, the donor may make contributions to the church designated for the insurance policy's premium payments. Here the church may have no option but to retain the policy. Additional insurance premiums payments to the life insurance company made either directly or indirectly by the donor of the policy may be acknowledged with charitable income tax receipts.

The church, however, should point out to the donor that better capital accumulation might result if the policy premiums and the additional gifts were, during the individual's life expectancy, invested outside the policy. This is because the church is not taxable on its earned-investment income, whereas individuals and corporations must pay income tax on the income of non-tax-sheltered investments. All of a church's investments benefit from the full effect of compounding investment income without reducing the annual earnings by the income tax that would have to be paid by individuals and corporations. Because charities' investment profits are not taxed, surrendering life insurance policy gifts for their cash-surrender value and investing the proceeds in other secure investments is probably better for the church's investment return than retaining these gifts.

Most donors will agree to let the church surrender a life insurance policy when the beneficial effects of doing so are explained. The church must, however, be sure to obtain the right to surrender the policy before accepting it. The gift's donor has no legal right to change the policy or the beneficiary once it is given and also does not have the right to change restrictions placed on the gift once it has been made (see the chapter "Designated Gifts" for further explanation).

Surrendering an existing policy is not in the life insurance company's best interest. The insurance company, therefore, might attempt to convince the donors that retaining the policies will produce a major payout if the donors should die long before their life expectancy. Although correct, the insurance company might neglect to explain the compounding effect of time (i.e., the policy value's rate of growth if the donor lives the average remaining number of years). Remember, most church members live lifestyles tending to extend their life expectancy rather than shorten it.

This chapter should not be interpreted as being negative toward life insurance or even the life insurance industry. Life insurance companies render a valuable service, and all should ensure their loved ones have sufficient financial protection. The promotion of life insurance policies as investment instruments for charitable purposes is a concern, however. A church having received a life insurance policy gift should calculate whether retaining the policy results in the best investment return. Whether a church is acting as a reasonably prudent person if it does not surrender life insurance policies for their cash-surrender value when that option exists, is to be determined by comparing investment income that can be earned if the cash-surrender amount were invested outside of the policy. See the chapter "Investing" for reasons why this is a concern.

Making the Church the Beneficiary of a Life Insurance Policy

Before 1998, to make a charity the beneficiary of a life insurance policy without also transferring the policy's ownership was not tax effective in Canada. The tax benefit of making a charity the policy's beneficiary could be used by its owner only if the estate was made the beneficiary and by including a provision in the will to have the policy's proceeds paid to the charity. This resulted in a two-step procedure; however, because the insurance proceeds had to flow through the estate, the insurance policy proceeds also became subject to probate costs and other legal exposures.

With the change in Canadian tax law in 1998, the insurance policy owner now can simply make the church the policy's beneficiary. The policy's proceeds will be paid directly to the church, thereby bypassing the estate and probate process. The donor's estate administrators can use the official receipt to offset up to 100% of income earned by the donor in the year-of-death and the year immediately prior to death.

Now that potential donors can designate the church as beneficiary of an insurance policy and still enjoy the related tax benefits, churches should discourage the ownership of insurance policies that are not paid-up.

Other Gifts in Kind

OTHER FORMS OF GIFTS IN KIND include various types of property that might be useful to a church itself or that can be sold for cash. For example, a church operating a second-hand store to raise funds for missions might encourage its members to make contributions, even of new products, the store will be able to sell. The church could accept any item delivered for resale as a gift. The only requirement would be that the church must determine, acceptably to the tax authority, the fair market value of such gifts in kind.

Gifts of Property vs. Gifts of Services

A church may not issue income tax receipts to individuals for church-related volunteer work. No *property* is transferred when someone offers services to the church as a volunteer. No matter how valuable the volunteers' services are, nothing tangible is transferred by them to the church. The volunteers have not parted with any property, only their time is freely given.

The same issue arises regarding other services provided to a church. For example, a church member agrees to service free of charge the church's heating or air-conditioning system in exchange for an income tax receipt covering the service's fair market value, which is usually readily established. The church should not acquiesce, since no property has been transferred to it in the performance of this free service. The volunteer could be issued an income tax receipt for the fair market value of replacement parts provided in doing the service, since they are property.

Before churches issue income tax receipts for gifts in kind they should determine whether the gift consists of property or services. If it is property, a receipt may be issued, but not if it is a service.

For some the distinction between property and services is unclear. For example, an airline's offer of a free ticket to be sold at the church's second-hand store is a service. The airline does not give property when it offers to transport a passenger from point A to point B. The ticket issued by the airline is only evidence that the holder has the right to the transportation service indicated on the ticket.

A third party owner of an open airline ticket has, however, made a property gift when she gives it to the church for resale in its second-hand store, because she purchased the ticket and then transferred it to the church. The fact that she paid for the ticket changed it from an offer by the airline to provide transportation services to a passenger from point A to Point B to property. When the ticket was paid for by the donor it became a binding property contract (i.e. the donor paid for the right to occupy the seat). It is this right that is the property transferred to the church that the church can sell.

To settle whether something is a service or property, ask whether the donor (not the recipient) has the right to surrender the item for cash or other form of property having a determinable cash value. Using the airline ticket as an example once again, because the airline cannot do business with itself, it cannot redeem an open ticket that has not yet been issued. Once, however, the airline has issued the open ticket by transferring it without cost to the church, the ticket has property value equal to the fair market value of the paid-up transportation right it represents, and that value can be redeemed by the church by surrendering the ticket for cash.

Similarly, an accountant making an offer that the church may sell vouchers for free income tax preparation is not transferring any property. The offer is simply one to render a service in return for the surrender of a voucher containing the offer. If the church, however, auctions or sells the voucher to one of its members, the voucher becomes property (i.e., the service has been paid for). If the purchaser donates it back to the church, the church may issue an income tax receipt, not for the amount paid by the service's purchaser, but for the voucher's fair market value. The voucher for a service is property once consideration for the service has been paid because it has become a binding contract.

In summary, the church may issue an income tax receipt equalling fair market value for any gift in kind it accepts, as long as it is property and the church can use it for activities in pursuit of its charitable purpose, or the church can convert it to cash.

Please note that a church should also gratefully accept a service contribution, but not receipt the donor; otherwise it could have its rights as a charity revoked.

Paying Board Members

IN CANADA, PAYING ANY MEMBER of a charity's governing board is controversial. The practice, however, of having a senior administrative employee, e.g. the chief executive officer, serve on a charity's governing board appears acceptable in the U.S. Why the confusion in Canada?

Some Canadian legal experts argue that *Income Tax Act* wording stating that no part of a registered charity's income "is payable to, or otherwise available for, the personal benefit of any proprietor, member, shareholder, trustee or settlor thereof" means governing board members may not be paid. Other legal experts argue that a governing board member who is also an employee is not being paid as a board member, but as an employee. As long as the employee is rendering valuable services for the remuneration paid, such experts argue, the charity's income is not made available to the board member by virtue of such membership. Instead, the remuneration is for services performed by the board member to the registered charity.

The second approach does not appear to sufficiently take common law and trust law into account. Lawyers arguing that board members who are employees do not receive salaries for such board membership also argue that charities' board members are only fiduciaries with respect to the donors and possibly the members of the charity but do not have the duties equivalent to trustees.

Conflict of Interest

The reasoning in the chapter "Who Owns Church Property?" would seem to be more in line with those legal experts who argue that a member of the governing board of a charity are equivalent to trustees and that they may not obtain any direct or indirect income from those organizations. In discussing church property ownership, a comparison was made with estate executors. Everyone intuitively accepts that estate executors should not benefit from their dealings with the estates, unless specifically authorized by the will, by statute or by a court. The common law and the statutes of all jurisdictions state that self-dealing in such circumstances would be a conflict of interest.

Specific statutes (legislated law) regulating payment to an executor or trustee exist in every North American jurisdiction. The prescribed limits normally are not restricted by the number of hours the executor or trustee had to devote to estate matters, but rather by a percentage of the estate's income and capital. The reason for such a restriction is that the executor or trustee must work exclusively in the beneficiaries' best interests. The executor or trustee may not be in a position where more hours spent on estate matters would result in more income for the executor. To avoid even the appearance of conflict of interest, the common law forbids any payment to the executor or trustee. The specific statutes allow the executor or trustee to receive compensation, but it is not remuneration for the amount of work performed.

It seems clear that board members of charities have the duty to work exclusively for the best interest of the beneficiaries of the charity's charitable purposes. How is this trustee obligation different from those of estate executors or regular trustees of trusts? Isn't a board member who is also an employee (or a supplier of goods and services to the charity) not in the same real or perceived conflict of interest as the estate executor or trustee?

The legal experts espousing, based on the common law of charity, legal precedents and written legal opinions, that a charity board member may not earn any direct or indirect income by dealing with the charity in any capacity, unless permitted by a legislative provision in the charity's legal jurisdiction appear to be correct.

The U.S. also is a common law jurisdiction. The question is: Have common law and trust law issues ever been fully addressed in respect to the duties of charity board members? Has corporate law been too easily accepted in the U.S. as applying to charities?

On the weight of the evidence available, I believe that members of the governing board may not materially benefit from any dealings with the charity unless specifically permitted by law. I now want to discuss the implication of such a position specifically for churches. A church is also a charity. Its task is to use all of its resources for the advancement of religion. Income members of the church's governing board earn from the church is not available for the church's ministry. That places the board members in conflict of interest with their trustee duties which require them to apply all the resources of the church to its religious purpose.

This conclusion might be perceived to cause difficulties for churches whose pastors are expected to be their leaders in all respects. The pastors, sometimes together with the elders or deacons, are to have spiritual oversight over the church. How can the seemingly contradictory issues of the pastor, needing to earn income to look after personal and family needs and being the flock's chief shepherd while an employee of the church be reconciled?

The Dual-Board Structure

The basis for a solution to the above dilemma can be found in the New Testament. When the apostles concluded that they were not able to spend enough time on their spiritual leadership duties because they found themselves bogged down with material issues, they decided to have deacons elected. The deacons' task would be to look after the church's material affairs (i.e., caring for the widows, the orphans, the poor and likely also other resource issues). The apostles were then able to devote all their time to the church's spiritual well-being and advancing the gospel to all peoples and nations.

If a church distinguishes between its two primary functions in its governance structure, the spiritual leaders could comprise the board of elders, and the resource administrators/trustees could be the board of deacons. (The terminology might differ in various traditions.) Both the board of elders and the board of deacons could be elected by the church's members, or the board of deacons could be elected by the board of elders.

If such a governance structure were adopted by the church, the board of deacons should become the legally-constituted board with the fiduciary and trustee duties regarding the church's income, assets and resource matters. The board of elders, including the pastors, would retain control over the church's direction, ministry and programs.

The concern of some church leaders regarding this governance structure is that the board of deacons could work at cross purposes to the board of elders. For example, the board of deacons could refuse to approve the budget needed to implement the ministry programs approved by the board of elders. In a church focussed on the same goal of service to its Lord, that should not pose a problem. If the board of deacons and the board of elders do not work together to implement the church's mandate, a greater problem exists.

If the possibility of irreconcilable differences between the two boards is a concern, the current unified governing board could elect a board of trustees from among themselves to become the legal governing board for property and finances. As long as none of the legal governing board's members are employees of, or do business with, the church, there is no conflict of interest between board members' fiduciary or trustee duties and personal income or profit.

Some Conflict-of-Interest Situations

As a final note on earning an income from the church on whose legal governing board one serves, a conflict of interest arises only when a member of the church's legal governing board either earns a salary from, or is in a business relationship with, the church, resulting in a direct or indirect real or potential profit to the board member.

Regarding purchasing goods and services, the response might be that no conflict of interest exists when the price was lower than another supplier's. This position is frequently supported by stating that all purchases are made based on quotations from more than one supplier, or based on price comparisons in the community. The issue in a potential court challenge, however, might not be whether the church received the goods or services at the best possible price but, more likely, whether the board member made a direct or indirect profit by providing the goods or services.

A church's board member, who is also one of its suppliers, whose donations to the church exceed the gross profits made out of dealings with it can not be accused of having profited from those dealings. This seems a better defence than the church's ability to show that the goods or services purchased from a board member were purchased at the best price possible. The church should, of course, always buy its goods and services at the best possible price. Potential conflict of interest, however, is between the board members' income from the church and their fiduciary and trustee duties as stewards of the public's interest in the charitable entity (i.e., the church).

To prevent conflict-of-interest problems from arising, avoid all conflict of interest. A church's employees and suppliers should not serve on the legal governing board responsible for the church's finance and material aspects. Such persons can, however, be members of the board having authority over the church's ministries.

Any member of the public can legally initiate complaints regarding the above-discussed conflict-of-interest situations to the appropriate authorities in the church's legal jurisdiction. The potential exposure to damaging press reports in itself is worth avoiding any conflict-of-interest risk.

Conflict of Pastoral Duties with Trustee Duties

A church dealing with whether a pastor should serve on the governing board looking after the church's property and assets should consider the pastor's real or perceived duties. A pastor is frequently seen not just as the leader, but also as the "father confessor." People come to the pastor with their needs, anxieties and difficulties. Even those not believing that the pastor (priest) can absolve them of their sins once they have been confessed, believe that the pastor should pray for and with them for the forgiveness of their sins. This means that the pastor might become privy to information that must be kept confidential, either at law or by common expectation.

If the pastor is also a member of the governing board responsible for the church's assets and property, the pastor must disclose to the other governing board members all information of which the pastor becomes aware that could have a material impact on the church's existence and operation. How can the pastor reconcile these two opposing sets of duties? To not place the pastor in such an untenable position is prudent.

Pastors should have the right to be notified of, and to attend, all meetings and to speak to all issues before the governing board. However, since they should not be members, they should not make motions and vote.

Where the church has opted for a dual-board structure consisting of a board of elders that governs the spiritual matters of the church and a board of deacons that has direction, control and accountability over and for the resources of the church, the pastor can be a member of the board of elders. In that kind of a division of duties, the elders do not have to share with each other or the board of deacons all information of which they become aware. As long as pastors are not members of the governing board, they are not subject to the duties applicable to a fiduciary and trustee.

Reimbursement of Expenses

Reimbursing governing board members' out-of-pocket expenses is not considered to be giving income to them. For example, if board members were required to travel by air to attend a meeting of the denomination or one of its agencies, they could be reimbursed by the church for the airline tickets' costs and related travel expenses. The board members do not profit from such reimbursements, but receive only a refund of what was spent by them on behalf of the church. No conflict of interest, therefore, can arise here. Reimbursements claimed, however, must be reasonable for the circumstances. They should be supported by invoices and expense vouchers where possible. Reimbursement of travel expenses when a private vehicle is used should be made at a reasonable mileage rate acceptable to the taxation authorities of the church's legal jurisdiction.

Paying Church Staff

A CHURCH AS A LEGAL ENTITY IS not able to perform its activities in pursuit of its charitable purpose without appointing volunteers or paid staff to do so. Effectively these staff are the church's agents, appointed to implement the church's programs and projects. This chapter will deal with financial issues in having paid staff.

Most churches hire at least a member of the clergy or a pastor charged with conducting the worship services as well as taking charge of the church's spiritual leadership. A growing or large church increasing its programs might hire more staff. Many churches have more than one person taking care of pastoral duties. No matter how many individuals the church hires, there usually are two classes of employees. The first class consists of those who are ordained, commended, commissioned, licensed or otherwise set apart for religious service according to practices of that particular church or denomination (i.e., those that are normally identified as clergy or regular ministers). The second class consists of those not set apart in any formal sense to perform religious services and are usually identified as non-ordained or support staff.

Regular Staff Remuneration

The church usually has two salary scales, one for each staff classification. The salary scale of the non-ordained staff is based specifically on a time commitment during the normal work day. Salaries paid must be reasonable in relation to the work performed. The church must be able to show that it is expending its resources exclusively to pursue its charitable purpose. For example, paying $20,000 a year to a staff member who is required only to take, print and distribute the minutes of the church's governing board likely would be considered unreasonable. Churches should determine a reasonable wage by researching what the pay would be for performing similar tasks and responsibilities in other organizations within the community. Another test of reasonableness would be to figure out what the governing board's members would personally be willing to pay to an "outsider" for similar work.

Clergy Remuneration

The reasonable remuneration of clergy members is a little more complex. Clergy normally do not have set hours of work. They usually are available to be called at any time of the day or night when emergencies arise. Not only are they preachers and teachers, but they are also counsellors and confidants for those in spiritual, mental and physical distress. Because of the multi-faceted tasks the pastoral staff deal with, maximum remuneration that can be defended as reasonable should be measured against earnings of professionals with similar qualifications and responsibilities. This does not mean a church should pay its pastoral staff based on salaries of professionals such as medical doctors and other health care workers. The point is that arguing the church is not devoting its resources exclusively to its charitable purpose based on the clergy receiving a substantially greater salary than the church's non-ordained staff would be difficult.

To also give the clergy and non-ordained staff the normal range of benefits is reasonable as well. For the clergy staff an additional benefit is the clergy housing allowance (U.S.) or clergy residence deduction (Canada).

Clergy Housing Allowance

The U.S. clergy housing allowance may be paid to clergy as non-taxable income. The non-taxable value that may be given to clergy living in church-provided housing as housing allowance is the home's fair rental value, including furniture and utilities. Qualified individuals receiving a housing allowance to rent their own home must be able to show they used the proceeds that year toward rent and utility costs. A qualified individual who is a home owner may receive the allowance to cover mortgage, tax, repair and utility costs. The allowance total that may be excluded from income may not exceed the home's fair rental value (including utility costs and the furniture's fair rental value). In other words, the American church must designate the amount paid to a clergy member as housing allowance. The clergy member is entitled to exclude from income only that portion of the allowance received from the church that is actually spent for qualified expenses within the fair rental value limitation.

Clergy Residence Deduction

Canadian clergy, as well as some other qualified individuals not normally employed by a church, do not receive a clergy housing allowance. Instead, each is entitled to deduct from income the fair rental value of the home one occupies. Canadian clergy may deduct the home's fair rental value and the cost of utilities that was included in their income if the church or other qualifying employer provided the housing. The maximum that may be deducted for those who rent or own their own residence is $1,000 per month for up to ten months limited by the home's fair rental value including utilities for qualified individuals earn-

EVANGELICAL MENNONITE MISSION CHURCH
BOX 234, AYLMER, ONTARIO N5H 2R9

ing $30,000 gross income from the qualifying source per year or less. The limitation of the deduction for those with gross income above $30,000 is the lesser of the fair rental value including utilities and one-third of gross income earned from qualifying employment. Canadian clergy are not required to show that the amount deducted as a clergy residence deduction was actually spent for housing in the year it was received.

A qualifying employer is either a church or a religious organization that has been designated a religious order for purposes of the clergy residence deduction provision of the *Income Tax Act.*

An individual who has the status of being a member of the clergy, a regular minister or a member of a religious order who is appointed by the denomination or the religious order to work in another organization or institution that otherwise would be a non-qualifying employer may also qualify to claim the clergy residence deduction provided there is sufficient connection between the purpose of the appointing body and the task to be performed on behalf of the non-qualifying employer. For example, chaplains in hospitals, prisons and universities usually receive their salaries from institutions rather than the church or denomination which appointed them. Pastors who have been appointed by their church or denomination for ministry duties at such institutions are eligible to claim the clergy residence deduction.

Historical Reason for Clergy Housing Benefits

The allowance or deduction is available to clergy because their functions in serving the church have been recognized as multi-faceted. Pastoral staff activities have been recognized as being beneficial to the community as a whole.

Arguments have been made recently that such benefits are no longer appropriate in a modern "enlightened" society. Critics of the historical benefit argue that most clergy now have offices in the church and that the home is used less and less for pastoral duties. Little or no evidence exists that the benefit is for the residence's use in rendering services to the community. That clergy have been entitled to the benefit because they were employed by the church to perform tasks the state could not do for the community is a stronger argument. Some of these tasks include spiritual counselling and confessionals, along with tasks supplementing state civic services like performing weddings. Such services were always done in the church rather than the clergy's residence.

The beneficial income tax treatment granted to clergy for housing is a cherished privilege. While the clergy housing allowance or clergy residence deduction exist, U.S. and Canadian churches are the beneficiaries of this favourable tax treatment. Most churches take this benefit into account when establishing remuneration totals for qualified clergy. Should this benefit be removed, the church would incur additional costs to maintain the pastor's net after tax compensation.

Staff and Volunteer Expenses

PAYING STAFF SALARIES IS NOT THE only cost of implementing the church's ministries and projects. In the process of delivering the church's ministries and projects, those who do this work for the church incur expenses on its behalf. Such expenses may include the use of a personal car to provide local transportation, e.g. the pastor visiting the sick. It may also include the purchases of minor supplies by Sunday school teachers.

Reimbursement for Supplies

With respect to minor supplies, the church will usually, but not always, reimburse the individual. It sometimes happens that the church does not reimburse certain out-of-pocket expenses because they exceed the budget amount for the particular project. When a volunteer or staff member does not receive reimbursement for expenses incurred to conduct the church's ministries, the amount is in reality paid by the individual with after tax dollars. In addition, the individual incurring such expenses on behalf of a Canadian church will have paid the GST/HST charged on the purchases of the minor supplies. (See the chapter "Goods and Services Tax" for more information about this Canadian consumption tax.)

As a general rule, the church should make certain that it approves the reimbursement of all expenses incurred by its staff and volunteers for the purchase of minor supplies. Even when the church is not able to budget a sufficient amount to reimburse all expenses, the governing board should authorize the reimbursement for all additional expenses subject to funds being available. By taking this approach the board will provide the staff member or volunteer with the option to make a special contribution to the church so that it will have the funds to reimburse the expenses. Such a reimbursement does not provide the donor with a benefit because the expenses were voluntarily incurred by the donor for the church's ministries. The donor merely has his financial position restored to what it was before the expenditures on behalf of the church were made.

Reimbursing Travel

Many churches provide a specific travel allowance to their pastors and other staff members. In the Canadian context paying a travel allowance is not very tax effective. Although the Canadian *Income Tax Act* permits the payment of a travel allowance to a pastor, the church must be able to show that the allowance was reasonable. The only way that the church can show that the amount was reasonable is to require the pastor to keep an accurate log book tracking all automobile travel for the church's purposes. If it cannot be shown that the allowance was reasonable (within the prescribed mileage rates listed below), the full amount must be included in the pastor's taxable income. In such an event, the pastor might not be able to claim personal travel expenses when filing the income tax return unless certain requirements are met.

Instead of paying a travel allowance, or providing the pastor with a church owned car, the most tax effective way to provide the pastor with a travel allowance is to reimburse the actual mileage driven on behalf of the church on a monthly basis. In

Canada the allowable reimbursement for 2001 is 41 cents per kilometre (45 cents for northern territories) for the first 5,000 kilometres driven in the year and 35 cents per kilometre (39 cents for the northern territories) thereafter. These authorized rates change on an annual basis by regulations published under the *Income Tax Act*.

Priority Payments

It happens that a church does not have sufficient funds to pay the pastor's approved salary and the expenses that may be incurred for travel, conference attendance and incidental supplies. In such situations there is a tendency to pay the pastor's salary and not to reimburse expenses.

As a general rule, the church should always reimburse expenses first. If the pastor's expenses are paid first, a number of things normally occur:

- The church does not have to pay its share of the payroll taxes, thereby saving some of the funds that will be needed for expense reimbursements,

- The pastor has more disposable income because less money will go to payroll deductions, and

- Canadian churches will be entitled to claim certain tax rebates only if the expenses have actually been paid. Rebates are available for GST/HST and a portion of the excise tax paid for gasoline purchases included in mileage reimbursements.

Benefits of Paying Full Expense Reimbursements

By reimbursing all supply expenditures and travel costs to all staff members and volunteers, the church accomplishes the following:

- It encourages the staff members and volunteers to be more generous by seeing to it that all appropriate supplies are available,
- It ensures that the staff member or volunteer will not pay for such purchases with after tax dollars,
- It will more accurately reflect the costs of providing its ministry services in its financial records and reporting, and
- Canadian churches will be able to claim the GST/HST rebate for such taxes included in the expense reimbursements for the supply of goods and services (e.g. the GST/HST included in mileage expense claims).

Designated Staff Support

THE CHURCH MUST DEVOTE ITS resources exclusively to activities exclusively in pursuit of its charitable purpose. In Canada the church must do the charitable work itself. Churches and other charities as artificial persons, however, cannot do charitable work. They need to implement their programs by appointing agents either as volunteers or employees.

Most churches use volunteer services to implement at least some of their programs. The rest of the programs are implemented by paid staff members. This chapter discusses special financial policies where a church remunerates its staff using designated funds received to support the work of specific staff members.

Gifts for Public Benefit

A church having more than one paid staff member either for its local or mission programs should have a clearly-defined salary structure. When a church pays a fixed salary out of its operating budget, establishing a salary structure is usually simple. Some churches, however, require on all or some staff to raise personal support (Canada), or to be involved in deputized fundraising (U.S.). Here the church establishes the programs and appoints the staff. The church, however, depends on the appointed individuals to raise the funds necessary to sustain the programs or projects, including payment of their salaries. This method of financing has a long history with mission organizations that are independent from any specific denomination. For independent and emerging churches to use such fundraising methods is also not unusual.

A variation of deputized fundraising or raising personal support in local churches is that the pastoral staff does not receive a fixed salary from the church budget. Rather, the pastoral staff's remuneration is paid out of designated offerings received either during or after the worship services.

Common to both fundraising variations is that the church's employees depend on designated gifts being received by the church to meet, as salary, their family and personal financial needs. For income tax purposes these staff payments need to be reported in the same way as when the church pays a fixed salary from the operating budget.

When staff members are dependent on support payments received by raising personal support or deputized fundraising, they do not all receive the same level of income. In addition remuneration might be erratic (i.e., gift income might not be constant throughout the year). This poses a number of potential financial challenges for the church.

The following situations might arise for staff required to raise their own designated support:

- Some staff will be more adept than others at raising financial commitments. Some might have stronger roots in the community, or might be better at presenting their ministry's opportunities and their personal needs to others. The church needs to assess the appropriateness of resulting unequal remuneration and whether that is conducive to the proper implementation of the church's mission and ministries.

- Individuals serving on the mission field who are financially dependent on their own fundraising efforts for their ministries might find that their support funds diminish over time. Consequently they might suffer such severe personal financial stress that they are no longer able to concentrate all their energies on the church's mission project, which could then become jeopardized to the extent that the missionary might have to return home prematurely. The expenses in shortening the service term might be unreasonable in relation to the mission project undertaken and the objectives achieved (or not achieved). Despite the missionary having to raise the required financial support, the church was the recipient of the gifts. The church must be able to show that the funds received for the mission project were spent efficiently and effectively for activities exclusively to pursue its charitable purpose. The church needs to consider whether emergency support arrangements should be put in place in such situations to ensure continuation of the mission project for a reasonable time period.

• Staff members who are very good at deputized fundraising or raising personal support might receive financial commitments that exceed a reasonable salary in the circumstances. For example, an individual required to raise financial support for his own project, might receive commitments far above what could be considered reasonable compensation compared to salaries paid by other organizations for similar work. To prevent this the church should establish a maximum salary that may be paid to staff members involved in raising personal support or deputized fundraising.

• Churches having staff members with salary limits set by the governing board often "bank" the excess designated gifts for future salary payments. Difficulties, however, could occur if such "banked" commitments cannot be paid for valid reasons in the future. For example, a staff member could decide to leave the church's ministry because of a move to another church or organization, retirement or even death. Funds designated for the support of a named individual may not be used for any other purpose. No person other than a court can change such designations (see the chapter "General Designated Gifts" for a general discussion on this issue).

- A church requiring individual staff to raise designated gifts for their ministry projects should request the following commitments from donors before accepting these gifts:

  a) The donor must agree that the contributed funds are for the church's ministry project (i.e., not for the individual's personal benefit). The individual who works to implement the project is supported out of the designated funds, but does not have ownership rights to the designated funds. A donation made and designated to a specific project must come under the church's exclusive direction and control to qualify as a charitable gift. Therefore, it is important to include wording similar to that in the chapter "General Designated Gifts" in all appeals.

  b) The donor must agree to give full control over the contributions made to the church so that if the project is terminated for any reason, the remaining funds can be used by the church for other ministry projects.

- Sometimes a church worker who decides to transfer to another church or missionary organization will ask that remaining funds in the designated project fund of the church be transferred to the new ministry that the worker is joining. The church should not agree to such a request. A church may not act as a conduit. Contributions are made for the church's ministry, not for the staff member's bene-fit and control; otherwise the donor would be involved in private benevolence and would not be entitled to an income tax receipt, because private benevolence is not considered to be charitable for income tax purposes.

Facilitating Personal Gifts

Occasionally donors making contributions to the church do so with the explicit direction that the funds be passed on to the designated recipients. This often occurs around Christmas time when a donor wants to send a special token of appreciation to a family member serving in a foreign-missions field. The contribution is intended to be over and above the normal salary that the missionary receives from the church or a mission agency that employs the missionary. The church needs to consider the following in this situation:

- The church does not receive control over the funds when they are directed to a particular person. In this instance, the church should not acknowledge the contribution with an income tax receipt. Such a contribution is considered to be private benevolence.

- Preferably, the church should not accept such a payment, but if it does and deposits the payment in its bank account, it will have to add that amount to the missionary's income unless it is satisfied that the contribution reflects a personal relationship between the contributor and the recipient (e.g., parent to child).

- Where the contribution cannot be related to a close personal relationship, the church would be required to report such amount as income to the missionary even though the contribution could not be receipted for income tax purposes.

- Funds deposited in a church's bank account are normally a resource received by the church for its charitable purposes. The exception is when the church can prove that it acted as agent for the private contributors, for example to facilitate the currency conversion and transmission of those funds. If the church cannot prove that it acted as agent of the contributors, it must spend the non-receipted funds for its charitable purpose and, consequently, it would have to disburse the amount as additional salary to the designated missionary. Such additional payments, however, would have to be within the maximum allowable annual salary established by the church for such a missionary.

Sometimes a member of the church wishes to make a special gift directly to the pastor. This happens where a personal relationship has developed between the pastor and a member. Such a personal gift does not relate to the pastor's employment by the church, but by virtue of the relationship that has developed. The pastor should not be required to report such payments as income for tax purposes.

Similarly, the church might decide to take up an offering to facilitate giving personal tokens of appreciation (i.e., a love offering) by members and adherents to the pastor and other church staff. To do this, the church should use the following procedures:

- It should be clear that the funds are not contributed to the church for its ministry and, therefore, no charitable receipts will be issued for such amounts.

- It should announce that any cheques should be made out directly to the intended recipient.

- It should return to the donor any cheque made out to the church, designated to benefit the intended recipient.

- Preferably it should not deposit the offering's cash or "loose change" proceeds in its bank account. Instead it should distribute such funds to the intended recipients directly.

By taking the above four steps, the church ensures it does not receive income for purposes that might not be considered charitable.

Paying Bonuses

SOME CHURCHES GIVE THEIR pastors and other employees a bonus, usually around Christmas time. The taxation authorities recognize this long-standing practice and treat it, with minor exceptions, as a regular part of remuneration. In spite of its common occurrence, some people question the legitimacy of making such payments and whether they are subject to any limitations.

These questions have no single answer. Each needs to be answered according to its specific facts. That people understand the principle discussed in the chapter "Who Owns Church Property?" is important. The discussion in this section presupposes an understanding of the fundamental question of church property ownership.

The pastor and other church employees are entitled to a reasonable remuneration for services rendered to the church. Because the church is required to devote all its resources to advancing its mission and charitable programs according to its legal objects, it might be required to give account regarding remuneration paid to its pastor and other employees. The remuneration must be reasonable and not conflict with the governing board's fiduciary and trustee obligations.

An example might help to focus on the issues regarding paying bonuses. Let us assume that a church involved in relief and development raises funds for a specific high-profile disaster project. The church is clear in its fundraising appeal that funds raised will cover administrative and other delivery costs also. In addition the church states in its appeal literature that it reserves the right to use excess funds for other projects at its sole discretion. While the church is involved in its fundraising program, a specific foundation announces that it will match every dollar raised from the general public with one dollar from the foundation. Because of this matching gift offer, the fundraising program is a huge success. More funds are raised than are required to complete the project. The church's management and staff are commended by the board for their excellent work both in raising the funds and in completing the project, and the board votes to use the excess funds to award each employee a bonus equal to the yearly salary. One of the motivating factors for the board's decision is that the church had not been able to give its workers a salary increase for the past five years. That the workers earn substantially less than they could earn in similar jobs in the government or private sector is generally recognized. The board considers that the one-time bonus payment brings the salary for each worker up to the average of comparable government and private jobs if considered over the past five years. Would such a bonus payment be appropriate?

The courts have given little guidance on this issue. A court in one jurisdiction stated that a bonus payment by a charity to employees who had not received sufficient salary for several years was a breach of fiduciary duty. The court's reasoning appears to have been that if the workers had rendered services for an agreed-upon remuneration, no further obligation exists to make subsequent payments. This reasoning suggests the church's board would not be devoting its resources to purposes for which contributions had been received by the church if it made these additional payments. To pay more for goods or services than the negotiated price or salary may not be considered as using the charity's resources appropriately.

If the board had previously asked the staff to continue their work despite the organization not being able to pay the salary to which they were entitled, the situation might be different. If the board had further made a moral commitment to the workers when salary reviews were suspended that they would receive additional pay retroactively when additional operating funds became available, the board would likely not be in breach of its fiduciary duty. Here the bonus payment would have been made to satisfy an earlier commitment when the staff performed services for less than reasonable remuneration.

When no clear commitment to pay bonuses to pastors and other church employees exists, not to do so is likely best. The church should put aside extra funds, if no obligation exists to make additional salary payments, and use them to provide future salary increases in the normal course of salary reviews.

Reasonable Remuneration

Even when a commitment was made to pay bonuses when additional funds became available, the church's governing board might be required to show that total remuneration, including salary, bonus and other employment benefits, were reasonable in such circumstances. The determination of reasonableness might be difficult. One test could be the amount the board as a whole would be willing to pay for the services rendered if their own funds were to be used. Another test of reasonableness could be to compare the salaries the church pays with salaries of those working in other similar service positions in the community.

The church is not required to pay the lowest salary, but if it were determined that the total remuneration package, including bonuses, exceeded similar service position salaries in the community, the church could expose itself to a breach of trust charge, even if the church membership had voted in favour of the bonus payment. Church members have no legal standing regarding fund disbursement beyond holding the board accountable to show that it used the funds for the purposes for which they were donated, as noted in the chapter "Who Owns Church Property?" Such disbursements must always be within the church's stated programs and objects.

Whether remuneration is reasonable is to be answered based on the common law. If more than a reasonable salary is paid to a pastor or other employee of the church, are the church's religious-purpose beneficiaries (i.e., the public) put at a disadvantage?

Love Offering

MANY CHURCHES FROM TIME to time invite missionaries and other speakers to conduct worship services or make presentations at special gatherings in the church. When these religious workers are dependent on raising financial support to be able to conduct their own ministry, the church might take up an offering during or after the service for the speaker's ministry. At times, such speakers are also residents of another country.

Under Canadian tax law, a church must devote all its resources to pursue its charitable purpose through activities carried out by the church *itself*. Under U.S. tax law, a church must see to it that all its resources are used for its charitable purpose. The significant difference between these two legal requirements is the italicized word "itself." To put it in different words, the Canadian church must do all its own activities to pursue its charitable purpose while the U.S. church need only assure itself that its funds are used for activities in pursuit of its charitable purpose.

Reasonable Payment Amount

The above noted distinction has a significant bearing on taking up a "love offering." A Canadian church can take up and pay a love offering to a visiting speaker only if the amount is reasonable given the services the speaker performs for the church, including conducting the worship services on a Sunday, teaching Sunday school classes or other similar direct services. If the speaker is known internationally, the reasonable pay for the services rendered would be greater than for a recent seminary graduate.

If a Canadian church has a visiting speaker employed by another Canadian registered charity having at least partially similar objects, the church could pay the full love offering to the other registered charity. A provision in the Canadian *Income Tax Act* deems payments made to another Canadian registered charity, called a qualified donee, as resources devoted by the charity to its own activities. Canadian tax law, however, does not extend that deeming provision to charities not registered under the Canadian *Income Tax Act*. Subject to a few exceptions a foreign charity is not a qualified donee.

A U.S. church is better able to facilitate a love offering. If a foreign speaker comes to a U.S. church, the church need only satisfy itself that the love offering will be used for its charitable purpose. As long as the amount paid above a reasonable remuneration for services rendered is used for the individual's regular ministry that furthers the church's charitable purpose, a U.S. church's obligations appear to be satisfied under U.S. tax law.

If the donors to a Canadian church's love offering require an official income tax receipt, the church would have to receive the gifts as its own funds. If a large sum were collected in the love offering, the church might have difficulty meeting the "reasonable payment" test, so for the church to announce at the beginning of the service that the money to be given to the speaker out of the love offering will not exceed a certain amount would be prudent. The church should further announce that the excess amounts will be used in the church's mission or other appropriate program.

Church Acting as Agent

If, on the other hand, the Canadian church's donors were prepared to forego an income tax receipt, the church could take up an offering as agent for the speaker. Here the church normally should not deposit the love offering in its bank account but pass it directly to the speaker. Donors should be told that any cheques should be made payable to the speaker or to the speaker's ministry directly. If, however, the speaker's organization is a qualified donee, the church would be able to accept the love offering contributions and acknowledge them with official receipts.

Normally the church would avoid using its bank account to cash the cheques if it acted as agent for a speaker employed by a foreign ministry. The moment the church deposits any of these cheques into its bank account, an argument could be made that the funds have become part of the church's funds. If, however, the church makes it clear that the offering is being taken on behalf of the speaker, the church is acting as agent. If such is the case, it is a good idea for the church to open a temporary account. Such contributions and related disbursements should not be included in the financial reports. By using the agent approach, the church should have a reasonable argument that it is not the recipient of the love offering.

Withholding Requirements

The Canadian church should also be aware that under certain circumstances, it may be required to deduct appropriate withholding taxes from remuneration paid out of its funds not only to its employees, but also to its speakers, especially if the speakers are residents of foreign countries. The church is required to report the amounts paid and withheld on the appropriate government-prescribed information slips, so the speaker may claim a refund of the amount paid by filing the appropriate Canadian tax return.

When Canadian resident speakers are self-employed there is no need for any payroll or withholding tax deductions.

Canadian Church Love Offering Summary

In summary, a Canadian church wishing to take up a love offering should take the following steps:

- Determine whether the contributors wish to receive an income tax receipt. If not, take up the offering as agent for the speaker. Here the church should not cash cheques for the speaker. The speaker preferably makes such arrangements with another party that could include a member of the church.

- If the donors wish to receive an income tax receipt and the speaker is employed by another organization recognized under the Canadian *Income Tax Act,* the church should consider making a grant payment to that qualified donee.

- If the speaker is a self-employed Canadian taxpayer, it is a good idea for the church to request an invoice for the amount to be paid. Before the love offering is taken, the church should inform all potential donors about the maximum to be paid for the speaker's services and that excess amounts will be used for other ministry purposes.

- If the speaker is a foreign taxpayer or works for a foreign mission organization, the church should determine and announce the maximum payment out of the love offering that may be made directly to the speaker. The church should also announce the purpose for which any excess money will be used. The church should ensure that the appropriate tax amount is withheld and remitted to the Canada Customs and Revenue Agency and that the appropriate tax information slip is issued to the speaker at the end of the year.

Short-Term Mission Projects

CHURCHES COMMONLY CONDUCT short-term mission projects serving purposes like the following:

- To implement part of every church's calling to go out and present the Gospel to all nations and people;

- To expose church members, usually young people, to the plight of those less fortunate; and

- To serve as a preliminary-exposure program for those considering a long-term missions service calling.

Mission organizations report that the short-term mission exposure is a good preliminary evaluation program, saving the cost of training and preparing those who believe that they might be called to serve in long-term missions but who decide to abandon the work after experiencing its realities. Although the merits of short-term mission projects will not be discussed here, the relevant financial issues will be outlined.

Church-Operated Projects

How to fund short-term mission projects is a frequent question, because normally their costs are not reflected in annual church budgets. A group willing to go on a short-term missions project is usually required by the church to be involved in raising personal support covering all costs, including travel, food and shelter for the participants as well as any goods and services needed to complete the project. Whether a contribution made by a participant's immediate family member toward covering these costs qualifies as a charitable gift is often asked.

The answer depends on direction, control and accountability. If the project is the church's own, as shown in the governing board's minutes, the church will have direction over it. If the church approves the project's scope and budget and agrees to pay all costs, subject to sufficient funds being raised, the church is in control. If the church also requires complete reporting and accounting of the project upon its completion, the church exercises full accountability over the funds used. Evidence of such accountability will be the incorporation of the expenditures into the church's financial records, and the availability of reasonable vouchers and reports to back up the mission project's expenditures. These three factors (i.e., direction, control and accountability) determine whether the project is that of the church. Failure to meet any of these three requirements would probably indicate that the project was only church-endorsed, rather than church-operated. Assuming the short-term mission project is church-operated, anyone should be entitled to be receipted for contributions toward its costs, including the participants or their close relatives.

The Personal Benefit Issue

Participants in short-term mission projects do not receive a personal benefit. They donate their time. That they are reimbursed for their travel and other out-of-pocket costs only puts the participants back into the same financial position they were before they agreed to serve. Such costs are incurred in rendering mission services. The mission activity is exclusively for the spiritual and material benefit of the people who are the objects of the short-term mission project.

Some might argue that the participants also benefit, because they learn to be more appreciative of the plight of the less fortunate. Such a benefit, however, is not a material benefit, but a moral one which might cause the participants to be more generous to the less fortunate in the future. It might also help them become better citizens, because of a better appreciation of democracy. And finally, it may lead them to a career of spiritual and social service to fellow human beings.

Personal benefit would result to the extent that the trip afforded the participants "vacation time." For example, if the actual mission project takes seven days to complete but the participants stay an additional week for sight-seeing and other personal activities, only 50% of the overall costs would be for ministry purposes. The other 50% should be paid by the participants personally.

Provided no personal benefit exists, anyone, including participants donating their costs, should be able to make a charitable gift toward covering project costs. As noted, such contributions would be for the project's recipients' benefit.

Church-Endorsed Projects

If a Canadian church does not operate, but only endorses, the short-term mission project, the church may not give income tax receipts for any gift designated for the project. A U.S. church, on the other hand, might be able to issue charitable receipts in similar circumstances. As stated elsewhere in this book, a Canadian church must devote all its resources to activities carried on by *itself*, and such activities must be exclusively in pursuit of its own charitable purpose. A U.S. church need only be able to show that its funds were spent for charitable purposes. A short-term mission project is in pursuit of the advancement-of-religion purpose.

A Canadian church might be able to accept gifts for projects it endorses that are operated by another Canadian church or other qualified donee as defined in the Canadian *Income Tax Act*. In such a situation, the Canadian church will be able to send gifts designated for such projects to the other church or organization because it is a qualified donee. If, however, the other organization is not a qualified donee, no Canadian donor would be entitled to receive a charitable receipt for a contribution designated to the recipient church or other charity.

Providing Short-Term Mission Bursaries

A Canadian church might wish to send a member on a short-term mission program controlled and directed by a charity in the U.S. As mentioned, the church is not able to send support for the member to the U.S. charity, because, except for a U.S. college or university listed in Part VII of the Canadian *Income Tax Act*, a U.S. charity cannot be a qualified donee.

If the church, nevertheless, wishes to support a member who will be under the direction and control of the U.S. charity while engaged in the mission project, the church would have to have valid reasons for such individual support. One reason might be the church wanting to have one of its youth leaders gain actual mission experience while under the U.S. charity's direction and control, so he/she may better establish the church's own projects in the future. Another valid reason might be the church, wishing to encourage support for missions or encourage members to engage in missions as either a short or long-term career, requiring the member to report on the mission experience to the governing board and the congregation.

Provided the church has a valid reason for involving itself in the short-term mission project engaged in by its members, the church might be able to award them mission bursaries. The bursary recipients would be going out on behalf of the church for training and learning. A valid activity of the church is supporting members being educated or trained for future services to it.

Such an approach would not be acceptable where the individual sought to cover his/her short-term mission expenses that were incurred for primarily personal benefit. For example, there are post-secondary education programs which require the students to participate in a mission service project as part of the course requirements. Such an educational purpose would have priority over the actual mission purpose. The student participants would receive the personal benefit of course credit and, therefore, the church should not accept the secondary purpose for funding any portion as a mission activity.

When a church awards short-term mission bursaries to its members, it should require that the participants, upon returning from the project, report in writing on what they have learned and report verbally to the congregation in either the worship service or the Sunday school program. Such written and verbal reports prove that the church awarded the short-term mission bursaries for its own charitable purpose, rather than to simply make charitable funds available to its members without a valid purpose of its own. If the latter is the case, the Canadian church could jeopardize its charitable registration number, because it is not devoting all its resources to pursuing its own charitable purpose.

Bursaries awarded for any reason by a Canadian church must be reported on a T4A information slip, which must be given to the recipients to file with their income tax returns. If the bursary paid during the year by the church to any recipient is $500 or less, no T4A need be issued. Each bursary recipient must, however, keep track of all bursaries and scholarships received in the year from all sources, and if the total is greater than $3,000 for qualified education purposes or $500 for other purposes, the excess must be included in income, regardless of whether T4A information slips were received.

Long-Term Missions

THE CHURCH NEEDS TO UNDERSTAND the financial issues it might face regarding career missionaries. Mission work is the church's lifeblood. Not only is it a theological basis for the church's existence, but it is also the legal basis upon which the church is considered a charity. The fundamental principle underlying the church's charity status is the advancement of religion benefiting the public. This concept has developed over many centuries in the common law tradition of our British heritage. Because of this legal heritage, churches are exempt from tax on their income. In addition a gift made by individuals to a church that is a qualified organization in the U.S., or one that is a registered charity under the *Income Tax Act* in Canada, are eligible for deduction from income or for tax credits respectively.

To do its mission work, a church might appoint individuals to do it directly on its behalf, participate in the mission program of the denomination or support an independent missionary organization. Sometimes the denomination or the independent mission organization through which the local church wishes to accomplish its missionary activities is in a foreign country. For example, a Canadian church might be part of a bi-national denomination with local churches in both the U.S. and Canada.

The process and limitations of financing missionary activities will depend on the actual relationship between the missionary and the local church. Several possible arrangements are discussed below.

Denominational Missions

In this first example, a local Canadian church of a denomination with churches located in Canada and the U.S. is assumed. The denomination's head office is in the U.S., and the mission programs are operated out of the U.S. "head office." The Canadian church can participate in the denomination's mission program in a number of ways.

Church Project

The first method is for the church to appoint its own missionary to a particular project in the overall mission program. The denomination would assign the project to the Canadian church. The Canadian church would have to take complete responsibility for, and control over, the assigned project. The Canadian church would hire and pay the missionary the agreed-upon salary and make all required salary deductions and remittances. The missionary would report directly to the Canadian church, which would report on the project's progress to the denomination. The denomination would have only indirect communication with the missionary via the Canadian church. In this way, the Canadian church would meet the requirements of exercising direction and control over, and accountability for, the mission project and all Canadian funds spent in the process.

Agency Arrangement

A second method of operation would be similar to the first, but the Canadian church would enter into a written agency agreement with the denomination. The agreement would require the denomination to exercise oversight over the Canadian mission project on the Canadian church's behalf. The Canadian church would also hire and pay the missionary. The missionary, however, would communicate directly with the denominational office according to the agency agreement's terms. The denominational office would report fully on the project's progress to the Canadian church. By concluding and implementing such an agency agreement, the Canadian church also would be able to satisfy the requirement that it exercise direction and control over, and accountability for, all Canadian funds spent on the project.

A Canadian church may take responsibility for a mission project within the denomination's overall mission program, but the missionary appointed to the project is a U.S. resident. Here the Canadian church could also enter an agency agreement with the denomination. The difference is that the missionary would be an employee of the denomination and not of the Canadian church. All the missionary's direct reporting and accountability would be to the denomination, which would keep separate accounts for the Canadian church's mission project, and its reports to the church would include a line-by-line financial accounting for the Canadian funds spent on the project. The reports should also contain vouchers to support the expenditures on the project's behalf when appropriate. The Canadian church would accept the reports, reimburse the denomination for the funds spent on the project and include such payments as funds spent on its own mission project. This procedure also would satisfy the requirement that the Canadian church exercise direction and control over, and accountability for, Canadian funds spent on the project.

Joint Venture Arrangement

Another arrangement, more appropriate in a denomination having multiple local churches in the U.S. and Canada, is to have the Canadian churches join into some form of Canadian federation. The Canadian federation could be incorporated, or it could be established by a trust deed. The federation, upon establishment, would apply for charitable registration under the Canadian *Income Tax Act* as a charitable organization for mission purposes. Once the charitable registration number has been issued by the Canadian revenue agency, the federation, as a qualified donee, could receive all payments from the Canadian churches intended for the denomination's mission purposes.

The Canadian federation would negotiate a joint ministry agreement between it and the denomination's U.S. office. Establishing a joint ministry means that all U.S. churches acting through the denominational office agree to enter into a joint venture with the Canadian churches acting through the federation. The two bodies (i.e., the denomination and the federation) would each elect or appoint representatives to the management committee of the joint ministry and would agree to contribute financial and human resources proportional to a formula established in the agreement. Effectively, both the U.S. churches, acting through the denominational office, and the Canadian churches, acting through the federation, agree to transfer all mission programs to the joint ministry. The joint ministry reports and is fully accountable to each of the two participating organizations in the joint ministry. The joint venture's expenditures are incorporated into both parties' financial records and reports proportional to their respective resource contributions.

Such an arrangement also satisfies the Canadian revenue agency's requirement of direction, control and accountability of the Canadian federation over Canadian source funds. (A sample agency agreement and joint ministry agreement are included in the *Charities Handbook*, published by the Canadian Council of Christian Charities.)

Missions Through Other Organizations

The second example occurs when a Canadian church wishes to implement its mission program through one or more independent mission organizations in Canada. The following situations, among others, could arise.

- The church could send gifts received for missions to an independent Canadian mission organization. Canadian Income Tax Act provisions deem those funds as having been spent by the charity on its own activities. Under trust law, the church may implement its objects by sending money to another charity with compatible objects. The church's obligation to account for the spending of funds for mission purposes ends with the transfer of funds to the other registered charity.

- A Canadian church can participate in a charitable program with an independent foreign mission organization only if the activity can be carried out under an agency agreement or a joint ministry agreement. See the descriptions of these two possibilities under their respective headings above.

- Canadian churches are often asked to support independent foreign missionaries directly without an agency agreement or a joint ministry agreement. That kind of support is illegal. If the Canada Customs and Revenue Agency determines that the church does not use the above-described procedures to disburse funds, the church exposes itself to revocation of its charitable registration number, meaning it can no longer issue income tax receipts. Such revocation also means the church would face a 100% penalty tax consisting of all assets it owned on the date of revocation, less any legitimate expenditures and less any assets transferred to a qualified donee.

A church would not be entitled to accept or pass on a gift designated for a foreign mission organization, even if the church did not give the donor an income tax receipt. See the chapter "Grants to Foreign Charities" for more details.

U.S. Support of Canadian Mission Programs

In this third example, a U.S. church wishes to implement its mission programs through a Canadian organization. For a U.S. church to send money for missions to a Canadian church, denomination or independent foreign mission organization is significantly less difficult than for a Canadian church to send such funds to a U.S. church or charity. Unlike a Canadian church, under the U.S. *Internal Revenue Code* an American church is not required to spend all its resources for its charitable purpose carried on by the church *itself*. The U.S. church need only give account that the funds were spent exclusively for charitable purposes. As a result, any arrangement stipulating that the recipient foreign charity must report to the U.S. church how the funds were spent for mission activities seems to satisfy the IRS requirements.

A local Canadian church should obtain appropriate professional advice before it enters any arrangement with any foreign denomination or organization to work on its behalf.

110

Grants to Foreign Charities

CANADIAN AND AMERICAN CHURCHES sometimes receive gifts intended for a charity in another country. In addition churches sometimes wish to support mission or relief and development work in other countries out of their general funds.

U.S. vs. Canadian Law

Under Canadian income tax law, a church must devote all its resources to a charitable purpose carried on by the church *itself.* Under U.S. tax law, a church must see to it that all its resources are used for charitable purposes. The significant difference between these two legal requirements is the italicized word "itself." To put it in different words, the Canadian church must perform all its own activities in pursuit of its charitable purpose, while the U.S. church need only ensure that the funds are used for charitable purposes. An American church, therefore, would not likely face significant difficulty in making grants to a foreign charity.

Canadian income tax law imposes significantly greater restrictions on a Canadian church. The church must show it uses all its funds for activities carried on by itself exclusively in pursuit of its charitable purpose. It must demonstrate that it had direction, control over, and full accountability for, the funds until they are actually spent on those activities. For a more detailed discussion of these distinctions and how the Canadian church can comply with its legal requirements, see the chapter "Long-Term Missions."

Outside the permitted methods of being involved in foreign activities in pursuit of its charitable purpose, a Canadian church is not normally allowed to send funds to foreign charities. Usually a church should return to the donor contributions designated for foreign projects that cannot be accomplished through the methods described in the chapter "Long-Term Missions."

Exceptions for Canadian Churches

The exceptions to this rule are the numerous foreign organizations identified as qualified donees in the Canadian *Income Tax Act* Regulations. They include many post-secondary educational institutions and organizations to which the Canadian government has made direct grants in either of the immediately preceding two years.

The foreign organizations to which a Canadian church is most likely to make legal grants would be post-secondary institutions. To be included in the list of qualified donees in the Canadian *Income Tax Act* Regulations, the foreign post-secondary institution must meet the following criteria:

- It must be accredited by an agency recognized for that purpose in the institution's geographic jurisdiction.

- It must be an institution normally attended by a significant number of Canadian students.

- It must apply for listing in the *Income Tax Act* Regulations.

What constitutes a significant number of Canadian students which normally attend the foreign institution has not been defined. Based on those listed, any institution regularly admitting Canadian students would likely meet this requirement. The accreditation criteria would be based on the submitted documentation.

Many Canadian churches look to U.S. colleges and seminaries to train their pastoral staff. Institutions listed in the Canadian *Income Tax Act* Regulations can receive grants from a Canadian church. Churches wishing to support a foreign college or seminary not listed should encourage the institution to apply for inclusion in the Regulations.

Grants to foreign organizations by the Canadian government are rare and would usually go to organizations like the Red Cross resident in a country where a disaster has struck. Most Canadian churches would likely be inclined to support a religious relief and development organization in the country where the disaster occurred.

A church without the formal agreements discussed in the chapter "Long-Term Missions" can contribute to foreign missions or relief and development activities by giving to one of the many Canadian registered charities doing such work compatible with the church's objects and mission. Since all Canadian registered charities are qualified donees, the church will be deemed to have conducted its own mission or relief and development activities in pursuit of its charitable purpose through the receiving charity.

Conclusion for Canadian Churches

A Canadian church may not make grants to foreign organizations recognized as charities in their particular jurisdiction. If a Canadian church wishes to be active in foreign missions or relief and development work, it must do so through one of the following mechanisms:

- Do the work itself through its own employees;
- Appoint an individual or foreign organization to be its agent under a properly-prepared and executed agency agreement;

113

- Enter a joint ministry with one or more foreign organizations to combine the participating organizations' resources through a properly-written and executed joint ministry agreement; or

- Select one or more Canadian registered charities and fund the work they will perform on the church's behalf.

Designated Mission Gifts

MOST CHURCHES RECEIVE GIFTS designated for their projects or programs. The support of a church's project or program would probably not cause any taxation concerns in most circumstances. Canadian and American taxation authorities, however, seem concerned about gifts designated to support a specific missionary.

Deputized Fundraising - U.S.

In the U.S. deputized fundraising has long been accepted as a method of assuring churches and other mission organizations that long-term funds would be available to support mission projects undertaken by individual missionaries. Although gifts might be designated to support named missionaries, the donors in reality are supporting the mission projects undertaken by the missionaries, not the missionaries themselves.

Mission projects, by their very nature, must be undertaken by individual missionaries, who need to be able to meet the expenses, including salary and living allowances, of performing the mission service projects they undertake. All funds paid to the missionaries which are not reimbursements of legitimate out-of-pocket expenditures are employment income. Such income is taxable and subject to applicable payroll taxes.

Raising Personal Support - Canada

Similarly in Canada, many churches and independent mission organizations require their missionary staff to raise their own support. Although the Canadian terminology is different from deputized fundraising, the purpose and structure is the same. Normally before Canadian churches or independent mission organizations agree to send out new missionaries, they require that the missionaries have ongoing financial commitments to sustain the mission project they will be undertaking to ensure that it will not have to be abandoned for lack of finances.

Private vs. Public Benevolence

Some Canadian and American taxation officials regard the designated support for specific missionaries as private benevolence, meaning that the donors have direction or control over the use of their contributions. A contribution to a church or other charity is considered to be a gift under both countries' tax laws only if the donation is transferred without consideration flowing back to the donor. The argument is that a designated gift for a specific person's benefit results in consideration, because the donors determine the beneficiary of their contribution. These tax officials argue that contributions can be accepted as gifts for income tax purposes only if they meet the public-benevolence test. Public benevolence. means that the donor must transfer the gift to the charity, so the charity receives exclusive direction and control over the funds.

In response to these observations, the following factors would show there is no private benevolence in designated giving for mission projects.

- The mission project is that of the church or other charitable organization, which completely directs and controls it, and exercises accountability over any financial expenditures incurred in conducting it.

116

- Designated gifts for missionaries' support are not for their benefit; rather they are to benefit the mission projects of the church or mission charity, which are carried out by the missionaries under the direction and control of (i.e., the missionaries are employees) the church or mission charity.

- Since salaries or living allowances paid to missionaries are taxable in their hands, they receive no benefit because of making a designated gift. The salary or living allowance is in consideration of their services to the church or mission organization.

- As long as the church operates a mission project as its own, no discrimination should occur against anyone wishing to contribute, even if the missionary undertaking the project is related to the donor. This discrimination would be equivalent to denying the pastoral and other home staff of the church the right to make charitable contributions to the church by which they are employed.

- If the donor has no legal obligation to financially support the missionary, the donor is supporting the church's mission project without any consideration or benefit flowing back because of making the gift.

General Designated Gifts

ASIDE FROM CHURCHES RECEIVING designated gifts to support missionaries and projects, they might also receive gifts designated for a building fund or other specific programs. As long as these projects or programs are charitable, most professional advisors believe it is proper for a church to accept such gifts. Those responsible for receiving and depositing gift income in the church's bank account, however, should take a careful look at all designated gifts before accepting and depositing them.

A gift transaction between a charity and a donor is completed when property, usually cash, is accepted by a willing charity from a willing donor capable of making a voluntary gift. The gift transaction is not completed until the charity, e.g. the church, has deposited it in its bank account. Before doing so, the church, or its designated representatives, can make any enquiries considered appropriate regarding the gift. After the funds have been deposited, the church is bound by any restrictions placed on the gift by the donor.

Conditions for Accepting Designated Gifts

A church should not accept a gift designated for a project or program not yet approved by the church's legal governing board. For example, if the church accepts a gift designated for building

119

a new worship facility, it should satisfy itself that it has plans to build such a structure. If not planning to do so, it should not accept the designated gift without the donor agreeing to modify the restriction, so that the church will have ultimate control over the use of the funds.

Designated gifts can be used only for the programs or projects for which they were designated. If the church used the gift for another purpose, it would be guilty of misapplying restricted funds, and that would be a breach of trust. See the chapter "Who Owns Church Property?" for the consequences of misapplying funds.

To avoid accepting a gift having a designation that cannot be fulfilled, the church should make sure a statement similar to the following is printed on all church budget envelopes and all other financial support solicitation material:

The donor hereby authorizes the church to use the designated funds for other church programs if the program or project for which the enclosed gift is designated has been fully funded or if the governing board, in its sole discretion, decides that the program or project for which the funds are designated will not be carried out.

Such a statement will give assurance that all gifts made to the church come exclusively under its direction and control, and avoids any potential for accusations that it misapplied designated funds.

Church Policy on Designated Gifts

The church should adopt a policy for its counting committee, treasurer or any other person authorized to accept and deposit gifts in the church's bank account. The policy should contain at least the following:

- All designated gifts received must be segregated in the church's financial records from all other gifts and must be accounted for separately.

- Designated gifts must not be deposited in the church's bank until the following has been determined:

  a) the program or project for which the gift is designated has been approved by the church's governing board, and

  b) the donor has given the church the right to use the gift for other programs or projects if the funds are no longer needed for the designated program or project.

- Designated gifts not meeting the above policy statement's conditions must be referred to the church's governing board, so it can negotiate an acceptable designation with the donor and, failing that, reject the gift by returning it to the donor.

- A designated gift received via bequest that does not meet the above conditions should be returned to the estate.

Accepting Bequests

OCCASIONALLY A CHURCH RECEIVES a bequest having a condition that the funds be spent on a project or program the church had not previously approved or even considered. When any doubt exists that the bequest can be used for the designated program or project in the future, the church should be aware of its obligations when accepting it.

Changing a Bequest Designation

Once a bequest has been accepted, neither the church, the estate's executor nor the family of the deceased can legally change the designation. Only a qualified court in the jurisdiction where the will was probated has such power. A church that receives a bequest with unacceptable restrictions should return it to the estate of the deceased to avoid the cost of applying to the court to change the designation. The executor will have to apply to the court for the designation change, and the estate will have to pay the cost of obtaining such a variance order.

It is possible that the court will not approve a change in designation if it believes the proposed alternative is too far removed from the testator's intentions. If that happens, the church may be removed as beneficiary of the will, which is far better than accepting a bequest that could lead to a breach of trust charge should the funds be applied to a purpose other than the one designated.

Enforcing a Church's Rights Under a Will

A bequest to a church might be contested by others claiming that they have legal rights to be the beneficiaries. Reasons could include a disinherited spouse, child or other dependent. Whatever the reason for the challenge, a church has a natural tendency to want to abandon its rights in the estate in favour of these related persons. A church does not want to be seen as "greedy" by trying to collect from an estate at the cost of family relations.

A church, however, may be legally required to defend its right as beneficiary under a will. Unless the testator (i.e., the maker of the will) was not of sound mind at the time the will was prepared, it is assumed that the testator made the bequest with full knowledge of the consequences. The testator could have had good reason not to include a family member in the will. Evidence for an intentional disinheritance would be clear if the testator included the name of an individual and left that person a nominal bequest. However, it should be remembered that certain jurisdictions have legislation that requires the testator's spouse and dependent children to receive a share of the estate.

Whatever the circumstances of a bequest made to a church that is contested, the church might not legally be able to abandon it. As discussed in the chapter "Who Owns Church Property?", a bequest or other gift is not made to benefit the board or church members, but for the church's charitable purpose. Such a bequest is made to it on behalf of the public, and the church must accept it not as the ultimate beneficial owner, but as trustee. It is this trustee duty which may legally prevent a church from abandoning a bequest in favour of the person contesting the will, even if the contestant is a close family member of the testator.

Conclusion on Bequests

In summary, when dealing with unusual bequest issues, a church should seek legal advice from a solicitor or attorney specializing in trusts and estates. Such advice should be sought before a bequest designated for an unacceptable designation is accepted, or before a church abandons its rights and responsibilities when a will is challenged for any reason.

Borrowing for Operating Purposes

An incorporated church's governing documents usually include the power to borrow money and to incur debt, which all corporations are entitled to do to pursue their corporate objects. This does not mean, however, that legal restrictions do not exist on such powers. The discussion on church property ownership becomes crucial in understanding the circumstances under which a church corporation may exercise its borrowing power. In this regard, please read the chapter "Who Owns Church Property?"

Church Revenue Sources

A look at a church's operating fund revenue reveals three possible sources of income. The first consists of charitable contributions. These are trust funds as we have seen in other chapters. The second is investment income generated by investing surpluses or endowment funds. Such income is normally not restricted by a specific trust and is available for general church-operating activities. The third possible source of revenue is income from facility rentals and sales of goods or services, e.g. operating a day care or a bookstore. Such "business" revenue sources, although restricted to be used within the church's objects as found in the governing documents, are not trust funds subject to the law of trusts. The second and third sources of church income will be called "owned funds."

Since the first, and usually largest, source of income for the church (i.e., charitable gifts) consists of trust funds, it is a good idea to deposit these in a separate bank account. The trust funds must always remain in a positive balance. Despite what the governing documents might state, under trust law the church might not have the power to borrow money from the trust funds to supplement a shortfall in the operating revenues of "owned funds." See the chapter "Borrowing from Restricted Funds" for a more detailed discussion of this subject.

Borrowing Purpose

The need to borrow money for a short time frequently arises because of periodic low cash inflow. The church often receives the bulk of its gift income late in the year. Costs, however, are incurred fairly equally throughout the year. The operating fund often does not have sufficient reserves to cover all the church's expenditures during the low-income months. Consequently the church will routinely borrow money from the operating fund to pay bills during those months and replenish the shortfall out of gifts, investment revenue and other income during the high-income months.

Repayment of Loans

How the funds borrowed by the church will be repaid needs to be considered. If they are to be repaid out of gift revenue, a breach of trust law might occur. Whether current gifts can be used to repay operating loans is questionable. A gift is such only if the property transferred is used for a charitable purpose. The use of gift revenue to repay a prior operating loan appears not to meet the legal requirement that a gift must be used exclusively for a charitable purpose. This may be the case even if the original expense was incurred in activities pursuant to the church's charitable purpose. When an invoice is paid by a church using borrowed funds, the resulting loan is a transaction in its own right. The two separate transactions (i.e., incurring the expense and repaying the loan which was arranged to pay the expenses incurred) are quite different from each other.

Borrowing Security

A church is not legally restricted from borrowing money from a financial institution secured by its "owned funds." The church, however, must be certain that future charitable gifts are not placed at risk. This appears to lead one to conclude that none of the assets in, or future gift income of, the charitable gift fund may be put up as security for any loan debt incurred.

The church likely may borrow funds from a financial institution for its operating fund secured by revenue to be generated by the church's "owned funds." The corporation may also borrow money on the security of real estate (see the chapter "Borrowing for Capital Purposes)."

Complete Disclosure of Church Assets

A church borrowing money for operating purposes from a financial institution should ensure that it clearly discloses to the institution the nature of the assets listed on the financial statements. For example, if the church's net assets were $1 million, but half of these assets were trust funds made up of endowment funds, the church would have to disclose this to a lender. The financial institution would not be able to accept the $500,000 in endowment funds as security for any loans advanced, because those funds are not unencumbered assets of the church. In this example, therefore, the church would have only $500,000 of unencumbered assets it could pledge as security for the loan.

Liability for Failing to Give Full Asset Disclosure

The church misleads the financial institution if it does not disclose the true nature of its assets. The governing board's members might expose themselves to legal liability if the financial institution proceeds to advance funds greater than what is reasonable in relation to the church's unencumbered assets. If the loaned funds were not repaid according to the terms of the loan, the financial institution could attempt to recoup its funds by laying claim to the church's assets. At that time, the financial institution would discover that it could not realize the $500,000 of the church's trust assets.

This discovery would expose the governing board members and the officers of the church to legal liability, and the institution could lay charges to collect its loss from them. The courts would likely find that the church, its board members and officers misled the financial institution by willfully neglecting to disclose the church's true financial position.

Borrowing for Capital Purposes

BESIDES THE NEED TO BORROW FOR operating purposes from time to time, a church might also need to raise capital funds. Let us assume that the church wishes to construct a new place of worship which will cost about $1 million to complete. Let us further assume that the church decides it will proceed with the building program when at least 65% of the required capital funds have been received or pledged to be paid over five years. The remaining $350,000 will be financed. The construction program will be completed one year after the pledge campaign has been completed. The campaign will take six months to complete.

In such a situation, the church will have to finance more than the $350,000 that was not received in cash or via pledges. Let us assume that it will take five years to receive the $650,000 pledged in five equal annual installments. That means the church will have only the first two installments for a total of $260,000 in hand when the construction program is complete. The church's financing needs, therefore, will be about $740,000. The following table shows the borrowing requirement.

	Pledge Status	Cash Position
Total five-year fundraising result	$650,000	
First year cash received	(130,000)	$130,000
Second year cash received	(130,000)	130,000
Pledge and cash balances	$390,000	$260,000
Construction cost		(1,000,000)
Mortgage financing required		$740,000

Risks of Borrowing for Capital Purposes

In the previous chapter, borrowing funds for operating purposes was discussed. That a church may not put future charitable-gift income at risk by incurring debt was pointed out. A church borrowing money to construct a building, however, does not risk its future charitable-contribution income assuming the only security for the loan to build the new worship facility will be a mortgage on the church's real property. Why is a church permitted to obtain a capital loan, whereas an operating loan poses a problem? Does the church not intend to repay the mortgage primarily with future charitable-gift income?

Capital Property

Understanding property is important when dealing with such questions. As noted in previous chapters, property does not consist only of real estate. Property is anything of value received which can be surrendered or redeemed for cash. By its very nature, cash is also property, since it can be used to discharge liabilities incurred by the acquisition of goods or services. Cash gifts, therefore, are a form of property.

A church deciding to build new facilities exchanges one type of property (i.e., cash) for another type of property (i.e., real estate). This exchange does not constitute spending in the sense that the funds are consumed in delivering goods or services pursuant of the church's charitable purpose. Consequently a church financing a capital project is not using future gifts to repay loans obtained to pay for expenditures consumed in operating programs or projects. When a church repays a capital loan, it extinguishes a liability incurred to acquire a long-term capital asset. Borrowing to invest, assuming that the investment is one that a reasonable person would make in the circumstances, does not put future charitable resources at risk.

Since no legal impediments for a church to borrow capital project funds seem to exist, the best way to borrow those funds needs consideration. Several financing mechanisms may be used, including a conventional commercial mortgage, church-issued debt instruments such as bonds or debenture financing by members, bridge financing or a combination thereof. Each of these mechanisms is discussed below.

Commercial Mortgages

A church can obtain a conventional mortgage from a mortgage lender or other financial institution. A church choosing this method of financing should carefully consider the repayment structure. In the earlier example where the church conducted a capital-fundraising campaign to cover about 65% of the new-facility-construction cost, the church would have to finance about $740,000 when the construction was completed. This larger financing requirement was due to the fundraising campaign having resulted in pledges collectable over five years.

The church choosing a commercial mortgage financing method needs to be certain that it has the flexibility to make larger principal payments at least during the first number of years while it waits for the pledge collections. Better yet, the church should try to arrange an open mortgage. An open mortgage does not restrict the principal that may be included in any periodic payment.

The advantage of a standard commercial mortgage is that the church knows the amount that needs to be budgeted as payments for mortgage principal and interest payments. Such a mortgage assures the church that the required payments will remain constant for the selected term, usually five years.

The security of knowing that the interest rate will not change over the selected term of the mortgage increases the risk for the lender. Consequently the lender will add a risk factor to the interest rate. Mortgage interest rates usually are higher for longer terms. For example, a mortgage amortized over 25 years with an initial one-year term may be available at one or two percentage points less than if the initial term is ten years.

In addition to the risks mortgage lenders associate with a longer-term mortgage, commercial mortgage risks are considered greater than those of residential mortgages. The theory, often supported by historical statistics, is that a corporation is more likely to walk away from a mortgage indebtedness than a home owner. Unfortunately, church mortgages are normally classified as commercial. Risks associated with mortgage loans issued on church properties are, however, significantly less than those associated with properties used in business ventures. Nevertheless, a church is usually required to pay mortgage interest commensurate with the increased commercial risk.

Because of the real and imagined risk factors, a church usually is required to pay significantly higher interest rates than those applied to residential properties. At least for the $390,000 for which it has firm pledges in hand, the church might not wish to pay higher interest rates. The solution might be to arrange bridge financing with the church's financial institution or another lender.

Debenture Financing

Another method frequently used by churches to finance their capital projects is to raise the funds via debentures or bonds. The debentures or bonds would be created by a church and purchased by its members and adherents. Usually some confusion occurs as to how to go about establishing such a debenture or bond financing system. For the remainder of this discussion, only debenture financing will be referred to, although no significant difference exists between the two.

To better understand debenture financing considering the security that might be used is helpful. In commercial situations, corporations often issue debentures secured by a general charge against all the corporation's assets. As was discussed in the previous chapter a church should secure operating loans only with assets derived from other than gift revenue. A church, consequently, would be able to secure debenture financing with future contribution income or with its capital assets. Since in the earlier example the debenture financing would be required to finance the church's new worship facilities, the capital assets should be used to secure the debentures issued to the members and adherents.

The ideal security structure for issuing debentures would thus be to mortgage the church's real property and break the mortgage into small parts called debenture units. These could be issued in any multiples, but usually they would be in multiples of $100 or $1,000. To accomplish this the church would appoint a trustee to hold the mortgage on behalf of all the debenture holders. The mortgage document would be drafted in such a way that a minimum and a maximum would be placed on the total to be raised through issuing debentures. It would also spell out the normal terms of a mortgage and describe the relationship between the trustee and the debenture holders. It would also describe the rights and obligations of the borrower, the trustee and the debenture holders.

Since the church's members and adherents are not concerned about some of the financing risks that would concern commercial lenders, the interest to be paid on mortgage debenture units usually is about two to three percent lower than their commercial counterparts. It might also be possible to structure the debenture section of the mortgage so that individual members and adherents can select a rate of interest on their particular debenture units that is lower than the maximum approved rate.

The trustee would collect all the debenture revenue from the members and adherents, and once the minimum had been subscribed for, the trustee would remit the funds to the church according to the mortgage's terms. To sell the debenture units over time is not unusual. Not all members wishing to participate will immediately have the cash they would like to commit to purchasing debenture units. The trustee should be encouraged to also obtain firm pledges for debenture unit purchases over the next number of years. Such firm pledges may also be used to obtain bridge financing from the church's financial institution.

An added feature could be included in the debenture mortgage instrument permitting the trustee to allow members and adherents to find replacement investors should they need to dispose of their debenture units. This will assure some members that they might be able to liquidate their debenture units instead of being required to hold them until the mortgage matures.

Member Loan Financing

A variation of the debenture unit financing might be where the members borrow funds from their own bank and make a personal loan to the church. To make certain that the interest paid on the loan from the bank would be deductible from taxable income, the member would make the loan to the church at a slightly higher rate of interest.

Bridge Financing

Bridge financing is frequently available for capital projects when short-term financing needs to be obtained until the long-term financing can be put in place. Normally such financing is available to cover the construction progress payments until the building is complete. Conventional mortgages usually cannot be put in place until the building is complete.

Even when the construction is completed it might still be possible to arrange bridge financing to finance the outstanding cash and mortgage debenture unit pledges. As long as the financial institution with which the church is dealing considers the church and its membership to be relatively stable and the members to have good credit records, continuing the bridge financing until the remaining pledges are collected should not be too difficult.

Bridge financing, since it is classified as short-term, normally is less costly than long-term mortgage financing. For a church to obtain such financing either at, or slightly above, the prime lending rate for loans issued to the financial institution's most credit worthy customers is not unusual.

Combination Financing

A church might not see its way clear to obtain all the required financing via cash, mortgage debenture unit pledges and member loan or trust financing. The church might then choose to use a combination of the financing mechanisms discussed above. For example, the church might conclude that it can raise 50% of the required capital costs in cash pledges over five years and another 25% by mortgage debenture units. That would leave the remaining 25% to be financed using a conventional mortgage.

Here the church would still require bridge financing to cover the period until all the cash and mortgage debenture unit pledges are collected. The financial institution providing the bridge financing, wishing to receive security for it, would possibly ask for a first mortgage on the church's real estate. The conventional mortgage lender would, however, also wish to have a first mortgage. If it is not able to obtain that, the interest rate the conventional mortgage lender would charge would be significantly higher. The solution would be to negotiate with the church's financial institution that it accept as security the cash and debenture unit pledges together with a second mortgage as sufficient security for the bridge financing.

If the combination financing method is used, the mortgage debenture would have to rank in third place after the conventional mortgage and the bridge financing mortgage. The members and adherents should not be too concerned about this situation, since the debenture mortgage will automatically move into second place as soon as the bridge financing has been repaid.

Borrowing for Restricted Funds

As NOTED IN THE CHAPTER "Borrowing for Operating Purposes," a church likely would not be legally restricted if it uses its unencumbered assets as security in obtaining a loan from a financial institution. The church must be certain that future charitable gifts are not put at risk. This would likely mean that none of the assets in, or future gift income of, the charitable gift fund may be used as security for any operating loan indebtedness. It also seems to mean that the church may not borrow money for operating purposes from other restricted funds it holds, such as an endowment fund or a building fund.

For the discussion in this chapter, it will be assumed that all the money in the endowment fund and the building fund was designated by donors. In other words, the money in the endowment fund and the building fund consists exclusively of externally restricted gifts.

If the church were to borrow money from the restricted funds, several things would happen. In the first place, the church could be risking restricted-trust fund property. Secondly, the church as trustee might be in a conflict of interest. Thirdly, the church could be guilty of misapplying funds, unless the restrictions placed on the gifts clearly authorized the church to make use of the funds.

Risks Involved in Borrowing

A church might not be able to pay back money borrowed from restricted trust funds. This could happen if the church's fund balance were decreasing annually due to operating deficits. That the church might be paying a higher interest rate to the restricted trust funds than could be obtained through traditional investments does not change this unacceptable risk. Even if the interest the church pays to the restricted trust funds, from which the church was not legally authorized to borrow, is higher than that paid by other investments, it might still not be commensurate with the overall risk. At a minimum, the investment by the trustee of trust funds would have to meet the prudent-investor test, which appears impossible unless the loan was backed by secure assets of the church and the rate of return met the fair-market-value test.

Inter-Fund Conflict of Interest

The church is in a conflict of interest when it borrows money from its restricted trust funds, unless the right to borrow was specifically given by the donors at the time that gifts were made, or unless it had such powers through specific legislation. If the church borrows money from its restricted trust funds in any other circumstance, the church is in a similar situation as an estate trustee (executor/executrix) who borrows from the estate for personal use. Intuitively one understands that such a conflict of interest may not occur. The same intuitive understanding should prevent a church from borrowing from its trust funds. Unfortunately, borrowing from restricted trust funds is not always seen by the church or its governing board as a conflict of interest.

That the interests of the church are different from those of the restricted-trust fund (i.e., the restricted program or project) is not generally understood. The church's general interest is to pursue the advancement of religion through its various programs and projects. The interest of the restricted building fund, for example, is to see to it that worship facilities are constructed, so more of the general public are attracted to become members, adherents or worshippers. Although the focus of both interests is religion, the purpose of the church's operating fund is the general advancement of religion for the public benefit, while the building fund exists to provide the facility allowing the church's programs and projects to be better available in the community.

Misapplying Funds

A church borrowing from its restricted trust funds without specific legislative authorization or permission of the donors at the time the gifts were made could be found by a court to be misapplying funds. In most jurisdictions, the church as trustee can invest only as specified by donors or as approved for trustees. In some provinces, the church must invest trust funds according to the prudent-investor standard.

Where trust investments are still prescribed, investments in the church's operating fund clearly are not permitted. For jurisdictions using the prudent-investor standard, the courts will determine which investments are appropriate. The courts normally would not get involved in this, unless a loss had been incurred. An investment which might have appeared reasonable at the time it was made might not be considered prudent when reviewed afterward. The old saying that "hindsight is twenty-twenty vision" applies here.

It is best that all churches refrain from borrowing from their restricted trust funds for operating purposes, even if the donors authorize such borrowing. If a court finds a church has misapplied funds, the board members may be required to replace those funds from their own pockets. These forced payments would not be gifts eligible for deduction from income or for tax credits. Since a court would have ordered the board members to make the payments, the contributions would not have been made voluntarily and would thus not be gifts for income tax purposes.

Investing

MOST PEOPLE DO NOT SEE CHURCHES as being involved in investing. Every church, however, in the broadest sense invests its resources when deciding its specific purposes. Investment in its narrower sense is addressed in this chapter.

Most churches from time to time find they have a surplus in the operating fund. Some churches also receive gifts restricted for specific purposes such as a building fund. Until the operating surplus is needed or until the church has sufficient finances to proceed with the capital project, the money needs to be invested.

Qualified Investments

Traditionally investments could be made in safe instruments like government bonds, treasury bills or guaranteed investment certificates. Recently more sophisticated investment instruments have become available, such as index units, which track a specific stock index on a stock exchange, mortgage-backed securities, similar to government bonds and frequently guaranteed by government agencies, and other pooled-investment funds.

The emphasis in any investment used to be the security of capital. More recently, however, return on investment has become equally important. To invest in guaranteed investment certificates might be safe from a capital preservation point of view, but the investment return is low compared with investment returns of other instruments. For example, the investment returns of index units trading on most stock exchanges have been significantly higher than the returns on government-guaranteed instruments in the long-run.

Prudent Investor Standard

Added to the foregoing is the requirement that a charity must seek to utilize its assets in a manner which will maximize income at reasonable risks. In some jurisdictions certain investment instruments are declared permissible for trust funds by statute. In other jurisdictions trust-fund trustees are held to a prudent-investor standard, meaning basically that a church's legal governing board may be judged on its investment decisions by how a prudent investor would deal with personal funds in similar circumstances. This standard, if it ever becomes an issue, will be judged based on the historical information available. To predict the behaviour of future financial markets is impossible.

Investment Counsellors and Investment Manager

Because investing the church's restricted funds is complex and because of emerging standards that might be applied to a church's governing board, a church with significant capital available for investment should retain an investment counsellor knowledgeable in dealing with trust funds. This investment counsellor should advise the board as an outside expert. It should be noted that not all investment counsellors understand the special duties of trustees. The church board, however, must still make the final decision as to which investments to make. Such decisions cannot legally be delegated by trustees to others in Canada. In the U.S. delegation of trustee duties might also be a problem.

The investment manager would look after the church's day-to-day investments under the direction of the governing board or its investment committee. He/she should not be the same person as the investment counsellor. The reasons will be discussed below.

Need for an Investment Policy

Aside from the pure investment returns, the church's governing board will be concerned with other issues such as ethical investments. Before retaining an expert investment counsellor, the church should determine what other restrictions it wishes to place on the investment manager. The following example illustrates why.

A church board hired an investment manager in addition to retaining an investment counsellor, without placing any restrictions on the manager. The manager, thinking his performance was being judged by the investment return generated, invested the proportion of the capital designated for equity investments in blue chip stocks with significant dividend returns and good prospects of capital appreciation. A significant portion was invested in a tobacco company. The church's board was shocked when it discovered this investment when the first quarterly statements were received. The cost of unwinding the unacceptable investment was significant because of a market downturn that had occurred since the stocks were purchased. This example illustrates the importance of establishing a clear investment policy which will guide both the investment committee and the investment manager.

Investment Committee

Investing church funds can be very complex. Consequently not all board members have the desire or inclination to deal with such matters. The governing board, therefore, should appoint an investment committee consisting of one or two of its members and three or four members of the church having knowledge and experience in investments.

Investment Policy

The prudent-investor standard governing the investment of a charity's assets often includes a list of mandatory criteria a charity's board must consider in making investment decisions. Such guidelines are in addition to rules that might be relevant in the circumstances, such as ethical investment criteria. In 1999 the province of Ontario included seven such mandatory criteria as follows:

- The general economic conditions;
- The possible effect of inflation or deflation;
- The expected tax consequences of investment decisions or strategies;
- The role that each investment or course of action plays within the overall investment portfolio;
- The expected total return from income and the appreciation of capital;
- The needs for liquidity, regularity of income and preservation or appreciation of capital; and
- The asset's special relationship or special value, if any, to the purposes of the charity or to one or more of the beneficiaries.

Note that constructing new worship facilities might also be considered investing in capital assets. If that is the case the seven legislated criteria might also be applied to determine the prudence of such a decision.

Charity boards that do not consider each criterion to the same degree might have to demonstrate that this was prudent. That the above list is set out in the Ontario legislation increases the responsibility placed on individuals serving as charity board members in that jurisdiction at least. If, however, the legal experts who argue that the prudent-investor standard has always been part of the common law are correct, the above criteria might apply to all charities, at least in Canada. Charities' boards should, therefore, be able to show that they considered each of the above criteria. Failure to do that could result in exposure to liability for any losses incurred or for foregone gains.

Applying Ethical Investment Criteria

Ontario is not the only province that has or is changing its *Trustee Act*. For example, the *Trustee Act* of Manitoba was amended in 1995. That amendment dealt particularly with a protection for trustees who use "non-financial criteria." This raises an interesting point. To what extent may a charity include ethical criteria in its investment policies?

One legal expert in charity law has stated that the Manitoba provision raises the question whether, and to what extent, a "person of prudence, discretion, and intelligence . . . in administering the property of others" may take account of non-financial criteria in developing an investment policy or in making investment decisions.

British courts have frowned on non-financial criteria being used to make investment decisions. Charity boards might be able to use moral grounds in picking investments, provided that such boards are satisfied that their non-financial criteria would not involve significant financial risks.

For a secular charity to argue that moral or ethical criteria should override sound financial criteria would likely be difficult. Charities formed for purposes other than advancing religion would have a difficult time arguing that moral or ethical investment considerations should be an overriding priority.

The advancement of religion purpose, properly understood, presupposes a belief and value system that includes advocating the worship of God. Religion is advanced not only in assemblies, churches, congregations, parishes, denominations, synagogues, temples, mosques and orders, but also in organizations, schools, seminaries, and other entities engaged in activities to promote the doctrines, teachings, observances, and practices of such a religion, provided they are not subversive or immoral. Strong arguments can be made that advancement of religion means that churches must take into account moral and ethical considerations to be true to their calling. Churches, which have their roots in the scriptures of the Old and New Testament, have the primary requirement to teach and demonstrate loving God above all and loving one's neighbour as oneself. Put in another way, the moral and ethical rule, often called the "golden rule": "Do unto others as you would have them do unto you," has foundational meaning for Christian churches. It means that morals and ethics may not be ignored in any activity or decision undertaken by a church.

The Church and Ethical Investments

A church cannot claim it is based on moral or ethical principles simply by including such criteria in its investment policy. To show it is a religious charity, the objects in its governing documents should be absolutely clear that the church exists *exclusively* for the advancement of religion. Otherwise the church might not be able to claim that ethical and moral investment criteria should take priority over financial investment criteria. Investment decisions never become an issue until it is evident that an investment is not producing the returns desired by other people. Such an evaluation will always be made after the fact. Any member of the public can accuse a church or charity of making imprudent investment decisions, because the beneficiary of all registered charities, including churches, is the public.

Protecting the Church and its Board

Some jurisdictions still have the lists of qualified investments for trusts. As noted above, however, if those jurisdictions amending their legislation are only bringing them in line with the existing common law, the prudent-investor standard could be argued to be applicable in all the common law jurisdictions. Based on this consideration, churches and their boards would act prudently by taking appropriate action to limit any possible liabilities.

Whether via possible future legal action, or subjective evaluation of the organization's investment portfolio performance by members, contributors and the public causing reduced donations, that churches' boards and officers will be able to ignore the prudent-investor standard and its related criteria with impunity is unlikely. To mitigate these new financial risks, a church that has surplus operating funds or restricted funds should take at least the following steps:

- Appoint an investment committee.

- The investment committee should be empowered and required to retain the services of a qualified investment counsellor who understands charity law and trust law and its implications for the charity.

- With input from the investment advisor, the committee should develop an investment policy reflecting each of the seven investment criteria listed above. Such a policy also should address the non-financial concerns, such as ethical or moral investment criteria. (The policy should indicate that the application of ethical or moral investment criteria to restrict investments should not be taken as authority to accept an investment portfolio mix resulting in materially inferior investment returns.)

• The investment committee should select an investment manager (i.e., a broker or appropriate financial institution) to look after the actual investment activities and to report the results to the investment committee and its investment counsellor in an agreed-upon format and on an agreed-upon frequency.

The above recommendations presuppose that the investment counsellor is a person other than the investment manager. Since an investment manager normally earns commission income from transactions in an investment account, he/she would likely be in a conflict of interest if also acting as the investment counsellor. The investment counsellor should be retained by the church directly and paid on a fee-for-service basis.

If a church takes the above approach in dealing with its financial resources not required for current operations, it will not likely be accused of not acting with the care that a reasonably prudent and intelligent person would exercise.

Permissible Activities

AS NOTED, A CHURCH MUST DEVOTE all its resources to activities in pursuit of its charitable purpose. The church's charitable purpose falls under the broad charitable heading "the advancement of religion." Some speak of the activities in pursuit of a charitable purpose as "charitable activities." An activity, however, can never be either charitable or not charitable. For example, if a church puts on a Christmas pageant, such an activity cannot be described as either charitable or not charitable within the objects permitted by the church's governing documents. If the activity is undertaken purely for entertainment, and admission fees are charged, the Christmas pageant would not be to pursue the church's charitable purpose. If, however, the same activity is undertaken for visually presenting the story and significance of Christ's birth, the activity is undertaken for the advancement of religion, which ought to be the church's sole charitable purpose.

The church is involved in many activities regarding the advancement of religion. These may include worship, missions, education, benevolence and the artistic presentation of the Gospel message. The nature and centrality of a church's worship and mission activities are well understood both from within and from outside the church. Most people recognize that without worship and missions, either at home or abroad, a church can hardly claim to be advancing religion.

Education Programs

The education and training programs which take place on Sunday or during weekday evenings certainly would be recognized by everyone as central to the church's purpose. Without educating and training the flock in the church's teachings and doctrines, the church would not survive very long. The focus of such education is to transfer the doctrines ("truths") of the religion to the next generation and to equip them to become qualified ambassadors for the Gospel. The same objective would hold true for a church's seminary or Bible school programs. Some, however, might question whether operating a Christian day school has the same objective.

For example, if the primary purpose of operating a Christian day school is general education rather than religious instruction, questions could be raised whether such an activity should take place as part of the church's operations. A school whose primary purpose is general education exists for the advancement of education rather than the advancement of religion. In that case, the school probably should be operated separately from the church. If, however, the primary purpose of operating a Christian day school is the same as that of the Sunday school program (i.e., to teach children the church's teachings and doctrines), the purpose of operating the school is compatible with the church's objects.

Scholarship and Bursary Programs

The church may also meet its education and training objectives by establishing scholarships and bursaries for those who prepare for the ministry or those taught in religious schools. Provided the church can establish these awards meet the test of public benevolence rather than private benevolence, they also appear to be charitable at law. Although a program like this is charitable because it advances education, the church awarding scholarships or bursaries does so exclusively for the advancement of religion in line with its objective to educate and train the next generation for pursuing its charitable purpose.

The advancement of education is just as charitable as the advancement of religion, but the purpose of the church is the advancement of religion rather than the advancement of education. Its objects, therefore, are likely restricted to those complying with the advancement of religion. When the church's education and training programs are for religious purposes, the church will not likely be challenged about its "indoctrination" activities in its education and training programs. If, however, the education program's purpose is exclusively the general education of children, it is unlikely that the church is complying with the common law definition of "education" if it also presents its religious beliefs and doctrines as "truths" to be assumed and accepted by the students. The same considerations would lead to the conclusion that a church may operate a day care centre provided it does so for the purpose of advancing religion.

Benevolence Programs

Another clearly valid church activity is looking after the poor, the widows and the orphans. The church undertaking these activities complies with its teachings. The Christian religion has always had two dimensions, contained in the summary of the law as stated in the New Testament. Jesus Christ said that the whole law and the prophets were based on the fundamental principle that God's people, the church, must love God above all, and their neighbours as themselves.

This dual commandment effectively states that the love and worship of God is meaningless if Christians do not love those placed in their path, especially those with spiritual concerns and people like widows, orphans and the poor with material needs.

153

In doing this the church, therefore, may operate a benevolence fund as a deeply religious activity for the advancement of religion, not for the relief of poverty for its own sake. The church must be seen to be doing what it professes and preaches.

Advancing the Gospel Through the Arts

Artistically expressing the gospel message is another example of a type of activity in which the church may be involved. As long as its primary focus is presenting the Gospel in a visual or auditory way, it is not promoting the arts, even if the performance or exhibition receives critical public acclaim. If, however, the primary purpose is to promote the arts or the artists for their own sake, such activities do not pursue a church's charitable purpose. The activity would not likely comply with the church's objects in its governing documents either.

Ancillary Programs

Most churches have ancillary groups operating certain projects or programs that are sometimes viewed as being autonomous from the church. One example is the Ladies' Auxiliary. Such a group normally exists to raise money for special projects for either the church's internal or outreach programs.

A church having these groups should be aware that they are part of its overall structure and activities. If the Ladies' Auxiliary would be truly independent of the church, it would be an independent business activity. The profits (i.e., the amount given by the Ladies' Auxiliary to the church's programs) would be subject to income tax if the group is independent. As an ancillary program of the church, however, the business activity is a related business activity of the church itself.

A related business may be operated by the church if all the activity's profits are used for the advancement of the church's primary purpose. If the Ladies' Auxiliary is a part of the church, all the profits earned from its activities belong to the church to be used for its charitable programs and no tax will apply.

If the Ladies' Auxiliary or any other ancillary group is part of the church, care should be taken that their financial reports are incorporated into the church's annual report and financial statements. Failure to do this could lead to the conclusion that the ancillary group is in reality a separate business.

Other Programs

The above are only a few examples of activities in which a church may legitimately be involved. Another example is that a church may engage in missions by having camping or sports programs. Before beginning a new program, project or activity, a church must always ask whether the purpose for engaging in it is the advancement of religion. If the answer is yes, the church is likely complying with its objects in its governing documents.

To be certain the church is engaged in activities that are charitable and comply with its objects, it should review its governing documents whenever a new program or project is contemplated. If the church is in doubt about the compliance of any program or project, it should seek professional advice.

Goods and Services Tax

CANADA HAS A CONSUMPTION TAX that is applied to the supply of most goods and services. This tax is called the Goods and Services Tax or (GST). Three Atlantic provinces call it the Harmonized Sales Tax (HST). No similar tax exists in the U.S. To deal with how this tax applies to churches is beyond this book's scope. The only issue that will be addressed in this short chapter is the rebates for which churches and other charities qualify.

Many expenditures made by churches in Canada for goods or services are subject to the 7% GST or 15% HST. Some purchases, such as basic groceries, are subject to a 0% tax rate. Other supplies, like banking services, are exempt from GST/HST. For most purchases, the GST/HST amount paid is identified on the invoice or sales voucher.

It is important that Canadian churches claim their GST/HST rebate entitlement because of being charities registered with the Canada Customs and Revenue Agency. Charities that do not have more than $250,000 in total revenue for two consecutive years and that do not supply more than $50,000 in annual taxable sales are not required to be GST/HST registrants. Neither are they required to collect the GST/HST. All services and most goods provided by a church are exempt from GST/HST.

A charity is not, however, required to be registered for the GST/HST to be able to apply for the charity rebate. Churches and other charities will receive a 50% rebate of the GST/HST paid on their purchases when they apply for it.

Most Canadian churches are aware of the GST/HST rebate provision and application procedure. Many churches, however, do not know the range of purchases eligible for the rebate. When the pastoral staff, the board or volunteers have out-of-pocket expenses in rendering services for the church, such expenses, if incurred in Canada, include the 7% GST or 15% HST. The church should ensure all these expenses are reimbursed so the 50% rebate can be claimed. The church should record the GST/HST amount included.

The exact GST/HST amount included in expense claims is frequently difficult to determine. For example, if the church reimburses the pastor for mileage at, say, 41 cents per kilometre, the 41 cents includes a GST/HST component, even though no specific invoice identifies the GST/HST. In this case the GST/HST can be determined by multiplying the total payment by 7/107 or 15/115.

The Canadian *Excise Tax Act* recognizes that most out-of-pocket expense reimbursements include GST/HST. The church may claim the GST amount included in the expense reimbursements if they were incurred outside of the Atlantic Provinces. For expenses incurred where the HST applies (i.e., Newfoundland, Nova Scotia and New Brunswick), the church may claim the HST included in the reimbursements.

Glossary

advancement of education: One of Lord McNaughton's broad categories of charity as stated in the *Pemsel* case. The other broad categories of charity are the *relief of poverty*, the *advancement of religion* and *purposes beneficial to the community, not falling under any of the preceding heads*. The four heads of charity are descriptive of what the law considers charitable; they are not a definition of charity. Activities in the pursuit of advancement of education are those which seek to discover "truth" and those designed to train the mind.

advancement of religion: Activities pursuant of the *advancement of religion* are those which worship God and those intended to teach the church's principles and doctrines to the members and adherents, and to gain converts to the church. The teaching activities in pursuit of the *advancement of religion* are not intended to discover the "truth" or to train the mind, but for proclaiming the truth, because religion already knows the truth. See also "advancement of education."

agency agreement: An arrangement whereby a church or other charity appoints an agent to implement an activity in pursuit of its *charitable purpose*. The agent is under the direction and control of the church or charity and must give full account, including expenditure vouchers and project reports, to such organization as to how funds were spent for the church or charity's *charitable purpose*. See also "charitable purpose."

arm's length: A concept stating a person cannot, or may be perceived not able to, act with independence of mind when a direct relationship by blood, marriage or adoption exists between members of a governing board. This has specific meaning for fiduciaries and trustees. See also "conflict of interest," "fiduciary" and "trustee."

beneficiary: A person who is to receive the *benefit* of an estate's property or a trust. *Beneficiaries* normally can be identified when the trust is established. The exception is a charitable trust, in which the *beneficiaries* are identified by its stated purpose. A charitable trust is, therefore, referred to as a "purpose trust." The courts have ruled that a purpose trust is not valid, except if it is a charitable trust. See also "trust funds" and "trustee."

benefit: Something received by a person, not because of a barter arrangement. Some confuse the difference in meaning between *"benefit"* and *"consideration"* by using them as synonyms. *"Consideration"* leaves the recipient in the same economic situation after as before the transaction (assuming a fair trade environment) while the recipient of a *"benefit"* is usually in a better economic position because of its receipt. See also "consideration."

charitable activities: A phrase used to identify a church or other charity's permissible activities. In reality no activities are either charitable or not charitable in themselves. The reason for undertaking an activity determines whether the activity is done for a charitable purpose. If an activity is undertaken for the *advancement of religion*, it is in pursuit of the church's *charitable purpose*. See also "advancement of religion," "charitable purpose" and "religious purpose."

charitable purpose: Purposes identifiable as falling under the four heads of charity: the *relief of poverty*, the *advancement of education*, the *advancement of religion* and *purposes of general benefit to the community which the law determines to be charitable*. See also "advancement of education," "advancement of religion," and "relief of poverty."

charitable registration number: Issued by the Canada Customs and Revenue Agency (formerly Revenue Canada) as evidence that the charity is registered under the Canadian *Income Tax Act*. A *registered charity* must include its registration number on all *official receipts* issued for income tax purposes. See also "official receipt."

charitable remainder trust: A trust established where a charity is the *beneficiary* of the *remainder interest* after a specific time or when the *settlor* dies. Normally the *settlor* retains the right to the income of such a trust before death. The *settlor*, however, may also appoint another person to be the income *beneficiary*. See also "beneficiary," "remainder interest" and "settlor."

church property: The income and assets, including the church facilities, which are held by the church to be used for its *charitable purposes* according to the objects in its *governing documents*. See also "charitable purposes" and "governing documents."

clergy: Individuals ordained, commended, licensed or otherwise set apart for performing the denominational or faith community's religious functions or observances. Such individuals, both in the U.S. and Canada, are entitled to exclude from income certain costs of occupying their home up to the maximum of qualifying allowances received or employment income earned. See also "clergy housing allowance" and "clergy residence deduction."

clergy housing allowance: Amounts U.S. churches and other *qualified organizations* are entitled to pay to *clergy* tax free. Clergy in the U.S. are not required to include these allowances as income to the extent they spend it on qualified expenditures during the year up to a maximum of their home's *fair rental value,* including utilities and the *furniture's fair rental value.* The allowance is similar to the Canadian *clergy residence deduction.* See also "clergy," "clergy residence deduction," "fair rental value" and "qualified organizations."

clergy residence deduction: Canadian qualified *clergy* are entitled to deduct from income an amount equal to the lesser of their residence's *fair rental value* plus utility costs and $1,000 per month for ten months, limited by the total employment income from churches and religious orders for those earning $30,000 in gross remuneration from qualifying employment or less. For those earning more than $30,000 in qualifying employment income the deduction is limited to the lesser of the *fair rental value* plus utilities and one-third of gross remuneration. The deduction is similar to the U.S. *clergy housing allowance.* See also "clergy," "clergy housing allowance" and "fair rental value."

common law: The *common law* is that body of decided cases to which courts look in determining how courts have dealt with various issues. If no specific cases exist on point, the court will look for specific underlying principles in the decided cases which will help guide the court to the right decision.

The *common law* is the English legal tradition which applies to most English-speaking countries that do not have a civil code as their legal foundation. Both the U.S. and Canada are *common-law* countries. The laws of five states and one province are, however, based on the civil code.

conflict of interest: *Conflict of interest* exists if a *fiduciary, trustee* or someone not dealing at *arm's length* with such a person deals with *fiduciary* or *trust property* in a way that might result in personal *consideration* or *benefit*. See also "arm's length," "fiduciary" and "trustee."

consideration: A word used to describe one side of a barter transaction. A person offers to transfer something of value (i.e., goods or services) in return for receiving property (i.e., cash or something else having comparable value to the transferee). For payments to a church, no *gift* is made if *consideration* is received in return. See also "benefit" and "gift."

contribution: See "gift."

deputized fundraising: A common term used in the U.S. to describe a practice whereby individuals set apart for ministry are required to *raise personal support* for the church's project or program in which he/she will be involved. The practice is intended to assure the church that funds will be available to sustain the project or program, and are not for the personal use of the individual raising the funds.

designated gift: Contributions to a church or other charity that are restricted by the donor for a specific project or program.

The church should ensure that the project or program is pre-approved. The church should also make certain that the designation does not result in *consideration* to the donor. See also "consideration" and "gift."

endowment fund: Contributions made with restrictions that the capital contributed may not be used for a church's *charitable purpose* either in perpetuity or for a particular period. Only the income generated as a result of the capital investment may be used for operating expenditures.

fair market value: The amount of a payment made within a reasonable period by a willing buyer to a willing seller for goods or services available for sale. The cost to the seller of a property or service sold has no influence or effect on the *fair market value*.

fair rental value: A concept relating to a clergy member being able to exclude from income the *clergy housing allowance* (U.S.) or the *clergy residence deduction* (Canada). The *fair rental value* in the U.S. is the rent to be paid on the open market by a willing renter to a willing landlord for a furnished home including the cost of utilities. In Canada the *fair rental value* is the amount to be paid for an unfurnished home including utilities determined on the same basis as in the U.S. See also "clergy," clergy housing allowance" and "clergy residence deduction."

fiduciary: A person responsible to deal with property on behalf of others. For example, one appointed as power of attorney has *fiduciary* duties to the person who appointed him/her and must avoid any *conflict of interest* in dealing with that person's affairs. The *fiduciary* may not *commingle* the property of the one who appointed him/her with his/her own. Neither may the person's power of attorney deal with the person's property as if it were his/her property. The power of attorney also may not do business on the person's behalf with anyone who is not dealing at *arm's length* with him/herself unless specifically authorized to do so in the document creating the power of attorney. A *fiduciary* is always accountable to the person or group that has appointed the attorney. See also "arm's length," "conflict of interest" and "trustee."

fundraising dinner: An event where a dinner is arranged to raise funds for the church's ministries. The dinner's participants are entitled to receive a charitable donation receipt for the payment or donation made in excess of the *fair market value* of the dinner consumed. See also "fair market value" and "split receipting."

general education: Education given by a *religious school* that is intended to provide skills such as reading, writing and arithmetic. Normally it includes education prescribed by statute or ordinance for publicly funded schools in the state, province, territory, region or municipality in which the school is located.

gift: A contribution with specific legal meaning when used in the context of charity. The courts have defined a gift to have taken place where a voluntary and irrevocable transfer of property (i.e., not services) has occurred with no valuable consideration having been received in return. For a gift to have been made, the donor must have had the ability and right to transfer the property, with all its rights, to a qualified and capable donee. If the donor is able to retain direction or control over a contribution's ultimate application or use, a right has been retained by the donor and no gift has been made. See also "consideration," "designated gift," "private benevolence" and "public benevolence."

gift in kind: A *gift* of property, other than cash, made to church or other charity. A *gift* of services does not qualify as a *gift in kind*. See also "gift."

Goods and Services Tax: A value added tax in Canada applicable to the supply of most goods and services consumed in Canada. In the Atlantic provinces, this tax is called the Harmonized Sales Tax.

governing board: The body having the legal responsibility for the church's income and resources. Such a body has been called the board of elders, the board of deacons, the council, the consistory, the board of *trustees*, the board of stewards or a combination of these. Whatever the nomenclature used in a particular church, the *governing board* must be identified as such in the church's *governing documents*. See also "governing documents."

governing documents: The original documents, as amended from time to time, that were used by the church to become established and to become recognized as a charity for income tax purposes. Such documents could be in the form of a declaration of trust, a constitution and bylaws, letters patent, certificate of incorporation or other nomenclature. The primary characteristics of *governing documents* are that they at a minimum identify the governing board's makeup and powers, the church's objects and purposes and the method of replacing governing board members. See also "governing board."

irrevocable trust: See "charitable remainder trust."

joint ministry agreement: An agreement between two or more independent charities to carry out activities in pursuit of their shared *charitable purpose* through a joint venture. Each of the parties to the agreement exercise direction and control in proportion to their respective resource contributions. Each party also appoints representatives to the joint venture's management committee in proportion to its resource contribution. Furthermore, the joint venture's financial accounts flow through to the respective parties in proportion to their contribution. See also "charitable purpose."

loan-back: An arrangement whereby a person agrees to make a *gift* to a charity on the condition that the person may retain the use of the property for a specific period or until death. Since 1997 such a property *gift* made directly to the church or charity may not be acknowledged with an *official income tax receipt* in Canada. See also "charitable remainder trust," "gift," "official receipt," and "remainder interest."

non-qualified securities: Under the Canadian *Income Tax Act*, securities including mortgages, promissory notes and shares of non-publicly traded corporations, which are controlled by the donor, or someone not dealing at *arm's length* with the donor, are classified as *non-qualified securities* when they are contributed to a church or other charity. They must be sold by the charity within sixty months, or must cease to be *non-qualified securities* within the sixty months, if the donor wishes to receive an *official income tax receipt* for such a *gift* at the time of disposition. If these securities are disposed of within the prescribed time, the value of the *gift* for *official receipt* purposes is the proceeds of disposition. See also "arm's length," "gift" and "official receipt."

official receipt: Charitable donation receipts issued by Canadian *registered charities*. Receipts which do not, among other prescribed information, include the *charitable registration number* and the phrase, "official receipt for income tax purposes" will not be accepted by the Canada Customs and Revenue Agency (formerly Revenue Canada) when filed with the income tax returns of individual or corporate taxpayers. Canadian *registered charities* also may not include information on the *official receipt* that is not prescribed in the Income Tax Regulations. See also "charitable registration number" and "registered charities."

private benevolence: The act of giving property, usually cash, to another person where the donor has personal control or direction over the selection of the *gift's beneficiary*. See also "beneficiary," "gift" and "public benevolence."

private property: Property of which the beneficial owner can be readily identified. Registration of title is not the crucial determinant, since such property could be registered in the name of a *trustee*, agent or attorney. Whether property is private or public is determined by the rights of its beneficial owner. See also "public property" and "trustee."

public benevolence: Where the control and direction over a gift's use is irrevocably transferred to a third party trustee, distinct from both the donor and the *beneficiary*, usually a charity. The trustee has the exclusive right to use the *gift* for activities undertaken in furtherance of its charitable purposes. See also "beneficiary," "gift" and "private benevolence."

public property: Property where the beneficial ownership is held on behalf of persons whose identity cannot be determined. Title of *public property* is held by a *trustee* on the public's behalf. See also "private property" and "trustee."

qualified donee: A *qualified donee* is defined in the *Income Tax Act*, Canada, among others, as a Canadian *registered charity*, the United Nations and its agencies, a foreign post-secondary educational institution listed in the *Act* and a foreign charity to which the Canadian government has made a contribution during the immediately preceding two years.

qualified organization: A U.S. church is a *qualified organization* under the *Internal Revenue Code*. This exempts a church from tax on its income, and donors to the church may claim contributions made to a church as deductions from income to determine taxable income. In Canada a church is recognized as a charity only when it has applied for and received its *charitable registration number*. See also "charitable registration number" and "gift."

raising personal support: Equivalent to American *deputized fundraising*. See "deputized fundraising."

registered charities: Under Canadian tax law charities resident in Canada must apply for registration under the *Income Tax Act* if they wish to be permitted to issue *official receipts*. The Canada Customs and Revenue Agency (formerly Revenue Canada) issues a *charitable registration number* to the approved church or other charity effective on the application date. If approved, the church or other charity is authorized to issue *official income tax receipts* for any *gift* it has received. See also "charitable registration number," "gift" and "official receipt."

related business: Activities in which a charity is involved that are classified as business activities if performed outside the charity. A business activity qualifies as a *related business* if it is in direct support of a charitable purpose or if substantially carried out by volunteers, and any profit derived from the activity is used exclusively for the charity's charitable purpose or purposes.

relief of poverty: One of the four main categories of charity. Activities in pursuit of the *relief of poverty* are those designed to improve the economic quality of life in the community. Such activities are not restricted to working only with those who are destitute; they can also include activities designed to prevent poverty. For example, designing and building an irrigation system for farmers in a given community can be an activity in pursuit of the *relief of poverty*. See also "advancement of education."

religious instruction: Instruction given by churches which deals only with biblical or religious issues and which is not at the same time intended to teach *general education* skills such as reading and writing. Generally, Sunday school programs and instruction activities in *religious schools*, focussing on Bible, church history, comparative religions, choral music and devotions would qualify as *religious instruction*. See also "advancement of education," "advancement of religion," "religious schools" and "general education."

religious purpose: The *advancement of religion* purpose. See "advancement of religion."

religious schools: Schools at the elementary and secondary level of education, frequently operated by churches, which have as their primary objective the *advancement of religion* rather than the *advancement of education*. Such schools teach either exclusively religious subjects, e.g. Sunday schools, or they have a combination of programs offering *religious instruction* and *general education*. See also "advancement of education," "advancement of religion," "religious instruction" and "general education."

remainder interest: The value of a *gift* that remains when the church or other charity receives the right to take possession of a property that was irrevocably transferred to a trust by transferring the title to the property to the trustee. A *remainder interest* in property might result where a *charitable remainder trust* is established naming the charity as the irrevocable capital *beneficiary* at a future date, frequently the death of the settlor. A *remainder interest* also might result from a *gift* of real estate where the donor, or someone designated by the donor, retains the right to occupy the real property for a given time or until the donor's death. A remainder interest's present value is established by applying an acceptable discount factor to the current *fair market value* for the time until control transfers to the charity or for the remaining years of the *settlor's* actuarial life expectancy. See also "beneficiary," "charitable remainder trust," "fair market value," "gift" and "settlor."

settlor: A person who establishes a trust, also called a *trustor*. See also "charitable remainder trust."

split receipting: The practice by U.S. churches and charities of including amounts for which the donor may claim a deduction from taxable income as well as amounts for which *consideration* was received on the same receipt. Such additional information is not allowed on *official receipts* issued by Canadian *registered charities*. See also "consideration," "official receipt" and "registered charities."

trust funds: All contributions or gifts made to a church are funds to be used for the *church's charitable purpose*. Such funds are impressed with a purpose trust. *Trust funds* should be held separately from funds earned because of sales and services. Although the church must use all its resources for its *religious purpose*, *trust funds* may not be used to secure loans for operating funds. See also "charitable purpose" and "religious purpose."

trustee: A person who, in addition to having all the *fiduciary* duties, has obligations to persons other than those who have appointed him/her. For example, an estate's executor has the *fiduciary* duties but is not accountable to the person who appointed him/her. The person who appointed the executor did so when a legal document called a will was created. To be able to exercise the duties as executor, the testator (i.e., the person who made the will) must have died. The accountability of the executor is, therefore, to the *beneficiaries* of the will to whom the estate's net assets must be distributed. Accountability to *beneficiaries* who are distinct from *settlors* or testators (i.e., those who appointed the executor or *trustee)* makes a person a *trustee*. See also "beneficiaries" and "fiduciary."

Index

advancement of education 140, 152, 153, 159

advancement of religion 13, 14, 17, 21, 67, 101, 105, 140, 148, 151-155, 159

Agency Agreement 106-109, 159

arm's length 15, 43, 48, 160

beneficiaries 15, 16, 20, 22, 23, 37, 51, 52, 57, 59, 66, 77, 94, 123, 124, 140, 160

benefit 13, 14, 19-21, 23, 25, 26, 29, 31, 33, 34, 37, 40, 42, 55, 58, 65, 66, 75-77, 87, 88, 100, 101, 116, 117, 124, 140, 160

bridge financing 133, 134, 136-38

charitable activities 151, 160

charitable purpose 13, 17, 20, 21, 33-35, 51, 59, 63, 66, 73, 74, 83, 85, 88, 95, 96, 101, 103, 110-113, 124, 128, 133, 151, 153, 154, 161

charitable registration number 20, 41, 108, 109, 161

charitable remainder trust 13, 51-53, 161

church property 13, 21, 66, 91, 127, 161

clergy 73-77, 161

clergy housing allowance 75, 77, 162

clergy residence deduction 75-77, 162

combination financing 138

commercial mortgage 133, 134

common law 14, 19, 25, 65-67, 94, 105, 162

conflict of interest 15, 66, 67, 69-71, 139, 140, 163

consideration 14, 19, 22, 33, 35, 37-42, 44, 50, 63, 116, 117, 163

contribution 13, 163

debenture financing 135

deputized fundraising 83-85, 115, 116, 163

designated gift 84-86, 115-117, 119-121, 139, 163

endowment fund 139, 164

ethical investment criteria 149

expense reimbursement 71, 79-82

fair market value 35, 38, 39, 42, 43, 45, 47-49, 51-53, 57, 61-63, 140, 164

fair rental value 75, 164

fiduciary 15, 16, 68, 69, 71, 91-93, 164

fundraising dinner 39, 42, 165

general education 25, 26, 29-31, 152, 153, 165

gift 14, 17, 19, 22, 33-35, 38-40, 42-44, 46-53, 55, 57-59, 61-63, 84-88, 92, 100, 101, 105, 110, 111, 115-117, 119-121, 123, 124, 128, 129, 132, 135, 139, 142, 165

gift in kind 43, 46, 47, 55, 61, 62, 166

golf tournaments 39, 42

Goods and Services Tax 157, 158, 166

governing board 13, 14, 16, 17, 21, 34, 46, 51, 65-71, 74, 85, 91, 93, 102, 119-121, 130, 140, 141, 144, 145, 166

governing documents 16, 35, 127, 128, 148, 151, 154, 155, 166

investment policy 149

irrevocable trust 51, 167

Joint Ministry Agreement 108, 109, 167

loan-back 167

love offering 88, 95, 96

non-qualified security 48, 52, 167

official receipt 35, 39, 40, 42, 45, 48, 49, 52, 96-98, 110, 168

private benevolence 87, 116, 152, 168

private property 14, 168

prudent investor rule 150

public benevolence 116, 152, 168

public property 14, 169

qualified donee 96-98, 102, 108, 109, 112, 113, 169

qualified organization 20, 105, 169

raising personal support 83-85, 99, 169

registered charities 39, 41, 65, 96, 105, 109, 113, 114, 169

related business 154, 170

relief of poverty 21, 154, 170

religious instruction 25, 26, 29-31, 152, 170

religious purpose 14, 16, 94, 170

religious schools 40, 152, 171

remainder interest 44, 45, 52, 53, 57, 171

salaries 73, 74, 79, 81, 83-85, 87

settlor 16, 51, 52, 65, 171

split receipting 38, 40, 42, 171

trust funds 127-129, 139-141, 144, 172

trustee 15-17, 51, 52, 65-67, 69-71, 91, 124, 139-141, 144, 172